A PRIMER OF STAGECRAFT

Also by HENNING NELMS

LIGHTING THE AMATEUR STAGE

BUILDING AN AMATEUR AUDIENCE

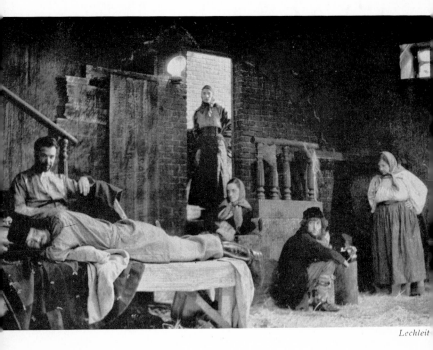

Lechleit

Details Used to Provide Realism

Corner of a setting for *The Harrisburg (Penn.) Community Theatre's* production of *The Lower Depths*. Designed by Edwin McKay.

A PRIMER OF
STAGECRAFT

BY

HENNING NELMS

Editor of *Stage Practice*

DRAMATISTS PLAY SERVICE

NEW YORK CITY

MANUFACTURED IN THE UNITED STATES OF AMERICA
BY THE VAIL-BALLOU PRESS, INC., BINGHAMTON, N. Y.

To HOFFER

ACKNOWLEDGMENTS

Almost nothing in this book is original. On the rare occasions when I have deluded myself with the belief that I had invented a new device, I usually found later on that someone else had considered it standard practice for years. Most of the material I have used came to me through Philip W. Barber, at that time Technical Director of the Yale University Theatre. The amateur stage owes Mr. Barber a great debt. He was the first to investigate the traditional shop-methods of scene building, and his analysis, *The Scene Technician's Handbook*, Whitlock's, Inc., New Haven, 1928, has been the source of nearly all the later work in this field.

Even as small a handbook as this could not have been compiled without the help of many friends. This help included supplying technical data and photographs, permission to use material, assistance in preparing the illustrations, and—perhaps most arduous of all—the reading of the manuscript and advice as to its phrasing and format. There is only space here to list names and to express my gratitude. I could wish for room to set out the contribution of each in full:

Albert C. Cloetingh, Director of Dramatics at Pennsylvania State College.

George Brightbill, Lawrence Peters, Marion Rauch, Kenneth Northup, and Edwin McKay, all of the Harrisburg (Penna.) Community Theatre.

Thekla Lockhart, A. B. Pierce, Jr., Marion Evans, Virginia Maddox, P.V. and Andrea Flynn, Fernand Pincoffs, Dorothy Dabney, David McIntosh, William J. McMullin, and Marian Kitchel, all of the Little Theatre of Houston (Texas).

A. W. Moellenberndt, and Billy B. Barnes, also of Houston, Texas.

Anyone who needs more information than this book and his own ingenuity can supply, should consult *Scenery for the Theatre,* by Harold Burris-Meyer and Edward C. Cole, Little, Brown & Co., Boston, 1938. This encyclopedic work deals chiefly with conditions in the commercial theater, but the advanced amateur will find in it a mine of information not obtainable elsewhere. I am indebted to its authors for a number of the ideas that appear here.

TABLE OF CONTENTS

PAGE

CHAPTER I. Scenery Is Simple 1

The Value of Scenery, 2; Technical Terms, 3; Outline, 3

CHAPTER II. The Stage 5

Directions 5

Permanent Equipment 6
Curtains, 6; The Inner Proscenium, 6; Rigging, 7; Background, 8; Traps, 9

CHAPTER III. The Nature of Scenery . . 11

Basic Principles 11
The Unit Method, 11; Materials, 12; The Plane Principle, 12

Typical Scene-Units 13
The Flat, 13; Draperies, 13; Natural Forms, 14; Steps and Platforms, 14

Other Classifications 16

Stock Scenery 16
Flat Height, 17; Flat Widths, 17; Openings in Flats, 18; Stock Drapery Units, 18; Ceiling, 19; Stock Doors, Windows, etc., 19; Stock Stairs, 19; Stock Platforms, 19

Economy Settings 20
Minimum Sets, 20; Convertible Sets, 22; A Three Year Plan, 23

PAGE

CHAPTER IV. PRACTICAL SCENE DESIGN . . 24

Drawings 24
> Drawing Equipment, 25; Floor Plans, 26; Elevations, 27; Sections, 27; Sketches, 27; Models, 28

Design and the Director 28
> Realism, 29; Location of Scene Elements, 29; Furniture Arrangement, 30; Platform Arrangement, 32

Technical Considerations. 34
> The Stage, 34; The Stock on Hand, 34; Cost and Difficulty, 35; Construction Methods, 35; Scene Shifts, 35

Sight-lines 36
> Horizontal Sight-lines, 37; Vertical Sight-lines, 38

Designing for Stock Units 40
> Numbering, 41; Assigning Flats, 41

Design Procedure 45
> Production Plan, 45; Rough Floor Plan, 45; Working Drawings, 45

CHAPTER V. TOOLS 47

Measuring and Marking Tools 47
Cutting Tools. 48
Driving Tools 49
Boring Tools 51
Gripping Tools 52
Miscellaneous Tools 52

CHAPTER VI. MATERIALS 53

Covering Materials 53
> Draperies, 53; Canvas, 54; Wire, etc., 54;

Gauze, 55; Padding, 55; Wallboard and Plywood, 55

Lumber 55
Lumber Sizes and Prices, 56; Woods, 56; Profile-blocks, 58; Molding, 59; Lattice Strip, 59

Adhesives 59

Hardware 60
Nails, 60; Tacks, 61; Screws, 61; Bolts, 61; Hinges, 61; Miscellaneous Regular Hardware, 62; Special Stage Hardware, 63

Rigging Supplies 65
Pulleys, 65; Rope, 65; Friction Tape, 65; Pipe, 65; Sandbags, 66; Casters, 66

CHAPTER VII. BUILDING METHODS. . . . 67
Carpentry, 67; Dismantling Scenery, 68

Hung Scenery 70
Drapes, 70; Borders, 70; Drops, 71

Flat Construction 71
Cutting, 71; Squaring, 72; Joining, 74; Canvassing, 75; Hinging, 78; Strippers, 78; Curved Walls, 79

Door and Window Flats 79
Sill Irons, 79; Canvassing, 80; Plugs, 80; Arches, 82

Cut-outs 82

Ceilings 84
Roll Ceilings, 84; Book Ceilings, 85

Doors and Doorframes 85
Doors, 85; Doorframes, 86; Hinging Doors, 88

Windows 89

PAGE

Bookcases 90

Fireplaces 90

Trim 92
    Molding, 92; *Papier-mâché,* 93

Platforms 93
    Legs, 93; Padding, 94; Cover-flats, 94

Stairs 94
    Stair Rails, 97

Irregular Forms 97
    Tree Trunks, 97; Rocks, 98

Repairs 98

Flameproofing 98

CHAPTER VIII. Scene Painting 101

Scene Paint 101
    Mixing Pigments, 101; Size, 102; Preparing Paint, 102

Painter's Equipment 103
    Brushes, 103; Pails, 104; Miscellaneous Equipment, 104

Pigments and Supplies 104

Color Mixing 106

Painting Techniques 108
    Flat Coat, 108; Spatter, 110; Scrumbling, 112; Sponging, 112; Dry Brushing, 112

Theory of Scene Painting 112

Painting Procedure 114
    Corrections, 115; Blending, 116; Texture, 116; Shadows, 117; Woodwork, 118; Snap-lining, 119; Wallpaper, 120; Stone, 121; Brick, 122; Leaves, 122; Convertible Sets, 122

PAGE

Washing Scenery. 123

CHAPTER IX. ASSEMBLING SCENERY . . . 124

Joining Flats 124
  Nailing, 125; Lashing, 125

Bracing 128
  Stage-braces, 128; Brace-jacks, 129

Stiffening 130

Placing Other Scene-Units 131
  Footirons, 131; Hinges, 132; Hooks, 133

Hanging Scenery. 133

CHAPTER X. SCENE SHIFTING 135

Running 135
  Handling flats, 135; Handling Doors, 136

Flying 136
  Rigging, 137; Knots, 137; Sandbags, 137;
  Counterweight System, 138; Drops and Bor-
  ders, 140; Rigging Roll Ceilings, 140; Book
  Ceilings, 142; Flying Back Walls, 142

Rolling 143
  Rollers on Platforms, 143; Rolling Jacks, 144

Routining a Shift. 146

CHAPTER XI. CONCLUSION 151

INDEX 153

LIST OF ILLUSTRATIONS

Corner of set for *The Lower Depths* . . . *Frontispiece*

PAGE

The stage house 7
Scene-units for a convertible setting 10
Cyclorama set—showing use of built units 15
Minimum set—showing use of draperies for borders and
    side walls 21
Interior sets 31
Exterior sets 33
Sight-lines 39
Rough working sketches 43
Wood-working hints—"Stage weights" 69
Structure of a plain flat 73
Canvassing and hinging flats 77
Door flats—showing plugs and plugging methods . . 81
Curved flats and arches 83
Doorframes, doors and windows 87
Fireplaces, bookcases, molding 91
Steps and platforms 95
Borders, tree trunks and cut-outs 99
Color-mixing guides 109
Painting methods 111
Drops, boomerang, snap-lining, and stencil 121
Joining flats—showing bracing and lashing methods . . 127
Stiffening methods, also picture frame-hanger . . . 130
Counterweight system, also useful knots 139
Ceilings and ceiling rigging 141
Rolling scenery 145
Shift chart 147
Stagehand's shift card 149

A PRIMER OF STAGECRAFT

CHAPTER I

SCENERY IS SIMPLE

Stagecraft requires less technical skill than almost any other worthwhile activity. Anyone who can handle a saw, a hammer, a screwdriver, a rule, and a square can build 99% of the scenery described in this book. If he takes the necessary pains his work will be, for every important purpose, as good as that of the expert.

It is this ease of accomplishment that makes scene building an ideal hobby. Everyone can take part; everyone can achieve results of which he may be justly proud.

Another pleasant thing about scenery is its low cost. Starting from scratch, a set can be built for as little as ten dollars, and added to, play by play, until a stock of scene-pieces is built up from which any type of setting can be assembled. Even in the best amateur theaters where the stagecraft is of professional grade, scene budgets are remarkably low. During my first four years as Director of the *Harrisburg (Penn.) Community Theatre* the scene cost was kept below twenty-five dollars a play, although the settings were often as elaborate as that shown in the frontispiece. Later, in *The Little Theatre of Houston (Texas),* with a total budget well over fifteen thousand a year, my scene cost rarely exceeded sixty dollars a show.

Yet if stagecraft presents so few difficulties, how shall we explain the obvious superiority of commercial scenery over the usual home-built article? The difference cannot lie in the taste, general intelligence or inventiveness of the builders. In these matters the union stagehand is usually inferior to the high school student.

The answer lies in the fact that scenery for the professional theater is built by men with a workshop tradition that goes back hundreds of years. Their methods have to be good enough for New York, and simple enough for the stagehands in a small town stock company. These methods were not invented, but were evolved through a long series of experiments and lucky accidents. The average amateur lacks this background and no amount of ingenuity can take its place. Progress is impossible without access to the knowledge that has been collected by generations of scene builders.

The purpose of this book is to make that knowledge available. It is based on the well-proven theory that anything within the capacity of the stock company stagehand will be easy for anyone else. I have made certain adaptations in cases where the requirements of the amateur differ from those of the professional. I have eliminated some fancy touches dear to the hearts of men who are paid by the hour. For the rest, I have tried to set down what I believe to be the best stage practice, whether for the country parish hall or the Broadway theater.

The Value of Scenery. Most amateur producing groups are fostered by the urge to act. The settings are regarded as a sort of fifth wheel—a necessary nuisance—to be wished off on the members of the organization who are "not good enough to play a part." Such an attitude is not only nonsense, it is particularly shortsighted nonsense as well. Scenery has an important effect on the actor. It sets a standard for his work and helps or hinders his imagination in direct ratio to its quality. An audience often judges a production more by its stagecraft than by its acting, if only because everybody can recognize well-made scenery while the difference between Leslie Howard's "art of understatement" and Willie Smith's stage fright is not always perceptible to anyone but the expert. Given good scenery, an audience is likely to say, "That was a fine play." With a slovenly set the most that can be hoped for is, "Weren't they all so go-o-o-d?"

Better scenery will win any group a higher standing in its community. It increases the range of plays that can be produced successfully, and will more than pay for itself in increased ticket sales.

There is still another point to consider. Actors are more

vocal than stagehands, but are they really more valuable to an organization? The answer to that is a decided "No." Statistics on leading amateur theaters show that the number of active members whose chief interest lies in back-stage work is definitely greater than the number whose chief interest is acting.

To sum up: Improved scenery helps an organization by its psychological effect on the actors. It increases the audience's approval and opens the way to better attendance and larger financial returns. Finally, it offers a new and varied field of activity and permits more people to take part.

Technical Terms. Every craft has evolved a special vocabulary for itself. The words of such a vocabulary designate frequently-used processes and objects. They save time and add clarity. If you have any doubt of this, try to rephrase the sentence: "Please fix the carburetor on my car" without using any technical words.

Unfortunately, the theater has chosen its terms with neither system nor intelligence. Many of them are awkward, many are inappropriate, and some are ridiculous. In spite of their faults, they are useful. I have included a number of them in this book and have tried to make the meaning of each clear when it first appears. The reader need make no effort to learn these terms. Those he finds useful will stick in his mind automatically. The rest he may safely forget.

Outline. The next few chapters are devoted to what may be called the practical theory of stagecraft. They will provide the reader with the basic knowledge needed for a full understanding of the hammer-and-saw practicality of the later chapters; but their principal purpose is to show how, by proper design, many unnecessary complications can be eliminated from scene building.

The chapter on tools is intended primarily for reference, and may safely be skipped on a first reading. The chapter on materials, however, is of basic importance, though you need not try to burden your memory with the numerous specifications and prices quoted.

The last four chapters constitute a how-to-do-it manual

describing in detail the methods by which all the common elements of scenery are built, painted, and handled on stage. Since these subjects are probably the chief interest of most readers, I have tried to make them sufficiently complete to cover any ordinary situation that may arise in amateur stagecraft. If, in the interest of thoroughness, I have included any device or process which seems too complicated for your present needs, you can salt it away for future use.

CHAPTER II

THE STAGE

Let us begin by examining the place where our scenery is to be used. The **stage house,** as we call the large room of which the stage is the floor, will influence our work in many ways. Its size, its shape, and its equipment will all make things easier or more difficult, depending on whether we take advantage of them or permit them to interfere with us.

The large opening through which the audience views the stage is called the **proscenium,** and the wall surrounding it the **proscenium wall** (p. 7). Directly opposite is the **back wall.** To right and left are the **side walls.** The corresponding walls of sets are also known as back and side walls. The areas on each side of the stage between the side walls of the set and the side walls of the stage house are called the **wings.** The space at the top of the stage house that is normally hidden by scenery is termed the **flies.**

Directions

Old-fashioned stages slanted downward from the back wall to the footlights. Modern stages are level, but we still use **downstage** to mean "toward the audience" and **upstage** for "away from the audience." **Above** and **below** are used with similar connotations. To say that an actor is below a table does not mean that he is under it, but rather that he is between it and the audience. The terms **stage right** and **stage left** are also survivals from an earlier day. They refer to the right and left of a person *facing the audience.* When we speak of anyone's real right or left it is necessary to say "your right" or "John's left" to avoid confusion. Such expressions are awkward but no satisfactory substitutes have ever been suggested.

The term **onstage,** which means "toward the center of the stage," is more logical. It occurs in such phrases as "move that chair onstage," and "only the onstage side of a piece of scenery is painted." The opposite of onstage is **offstage.**

Permanent Equipment

A stage should be equipped when it is first built, but this is rarely done and almost never done well. Only a small amount of equipment is needed, but without this the scene builder is handicapped from the start.

Curtains for amateur stages are usually of the **draw** type shown in the diagram. When funds permit, they should be made of velvet or velours. Since the curtains hang in folds, and must overlap on both sides and in the center, their combined width should be at least half again the width of the proscenium. Seams should run vertically. A lining of heavy black sateen will make the curtains light-proof and add greatly to their life. The tracks from which they hang should be equipped with rollers and should overlap 2′ 0″ or 2′ 6″ (read "two feet or two feet six inches") in the center. Track of this type costs from $1.50 to $3.00 per foot, depending on quality. It may be purchased from *J. R. Clancy, Inc.,* Syracuse, N.Y.

The inner proscenium is located upstage of the curtain and is the real frame of the stage picture. Since it must be adjusted to fit scenes of different sizes, it is made in three parts.

The horizontal member at the top is the **teaser.** In its simplest form this is a framework of wood covered with canvas. It should be painted heavily enough to keep the stage lights from shining through it when the auditorium is dark. The teaser is made adjustable by hanging it from a set of ropes, called **lines,** as shown in the diagram.

The sides of the inner proscenium are called **tormentors.** Besides their main function of hiding, or **masking,** the wings, these also provide a rigid support to which the downstage edges of the scenery may be attached. The most common type of tormentor is made by hinging two canvas-covered frames together like a screen.

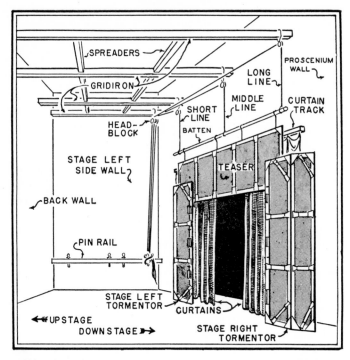

Rigging. Scenery hung on lines is said to be **flown.** Every stage should be equipped with apparatus for this purpose, as it is difficult to set even the simplest scene without flying a few pieces.

To avoid complicating the diagram only the teaser lines are shown, but in practice six or more sets will be desirable. Three lines make a set. Note that each line has its own pulley, or **block,** and that all three lines lead over the **head-block** which has three wheels called **sheaves** (pronounced "shivs"). From the head-block the lines lead down to the **pin rail,** where they are **tied off.** The pin rail is a heavy beam placed about 4′ 0″ from the floor and fitted with belaying pins like those used on sailing ships. The whole weight of the flown scenery pulls *up* on the pin rail, so it must be anchored firmly in place.

The rigging system is supported by the **gridiron** or **grid.** Where the grid is over 30′ 0″ from the stage it must include a lattice-work (usually of steel) on which the stagehands may walk while scenery is being rigged. This type of gridiron is very complicated, as can be seen from the example on p. 139, and must be installed by a professional rigging company. Lower gridirons are much simpler, but they involve a number of factors, such as the depth of the stage and the existing structure of the building, that call for the advice of a contractor or an architect.

If the ceiling joists of the stage house are exposed they may make an excellent gridiron. In cases where these joists are not strong enough, it is usually possible to reinforce them in some way. If the joists are not available, a grid of the type shown in the diagram may be installed.

A gridiron 30′ 0″ or less in height ought to be capable of carrying a total safe load of 1000 pounds. If it is weaker than this, a notice stating the safe load should be posted near the curtain rope. The four beams of the grid bear very unequal proportions of the weight of the load. For instance, if the teaser weighs 40 pounds, the beams supporting the **short** and **long lines** (see diagram) will carry only 10 pounds each. The middle beam carries 20 pounds while the head-block beam must take the whole weight of 40 pounds.

When weight is put on the lines they tend to pull the beams toward each other. The diagram shows how **spreaders** are inserted to prevent this.

Whether your gridiron is a steel worker's dream or merely a few screw eyes in the ceiling (p. 21), be careful not to overload it. There is a special providence that takes care of people in the theater. I have never seen a serious accident. But some day that providence is going to turn its back, and you should not be standing under an overloaded gridiron when it does.

Background. Wherever possible the equipment of the theater should include some sort of permanent background that can be used either as a sky, or as a screen on which lighting effects may be projected. If the back wall of the stage house is plastered, and not broken by doors or windows, the wall is simply given a coat of grayish blue paint. Even where the wall is concrete or brick, and a preliminary coat of plaster is necessary, the work should not prove too expensive.

If the sides and top of our plastered wall are extended downstage, and the corners are rounded out so as to make it resemble a hollow quarter-sphere, we have a **dome.** Wonderful effects are possible with domes, but they interfere with scene shifts to such an extent that their faults more than overbalance their virtues except for stages under 16′ 0″ in height. Here they can be recommended where funds permit. Domes are costly to build and are worthless unless designed by an expert.

Another form of permanent background is the **sky-cyclorama,** a half-cylinder of tightly stretched blue canvas hung so as to surround the playing space. These are supposed to have most of the advantages of a dome, and (as they can be moved out of the way) none of the disadvantages. My own experience is that once a season they are useful and the rest of the time they are a nuisance.

Do not confuse the sky-cyclorama with the ordinary, or drapery, type discussed on p. 13. The two resemble each other in size and shape, but they are different in appearance and function.

Other artificial skies are described on p. 14.

Traps, as openings in the stage floor are called, are desirable chiefly in theory. In practice they make the stage floor uneven, and squeak whenever an actor steps on them. Traps are almost never needed. When they are, it is always possible to build a platform and cut a hole in it rather than in the stage floor.

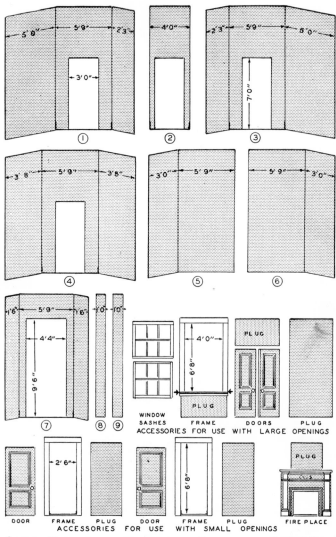

SCENE - UNITS FOR A CONVERTIBLE SETTING — 26'0" WIDE

CHAPTER III

THE NATURE OF SCENERY

The whole problem of scenery is simplified by the surprisingly limited number of objects that we are called on to represent. Nine tenths of all scenery is made up of architectural forms. Its basic elements are walls and ceilings, with doors, windows, bookcases, fireplaces, stairs, stair rails, and landings added as accessories. If we supplement this list with a few natural objects such as trees, rocks, and a sky, we shall have an almost complete inventory.

Basic Principles

Scenery should be economical and simple to build. When built, it must be sturdy, rigid, light, easy to handle, and capable of being stored in a minimum of space. If this seems an imposing list of scene virtues, I can assure the reader that it is by no means an impossible one. Let us glance at the principles that make such scenery possible.

The Unit Method. A scene is not planned as a whole but as a number of small units each of which is built and handled separately. From this point of view the scene is a collection of parts and resembles a watch that can be put together and taken apart, rather than a house that can only be built and wrecked.

As small pieces are easier to handle than large ones, the unit idea greatly simplifies the problems of building, shifting, and storage. Its chief feature, however, is the tremendous saving it makes possible in time and money. The use of a unit is not restricted to the set for which it is built. Suitably disguised with paint or applied ornament, the unit may be incorporated into future scenes and thus may appear in twenty or thirty plays. Since the first cost of the average scene-unit is around $3.00, this brings the cost per play (which is what really matters) well below a quarter.

Materials. We cannot expect our scene-units to last unless we build them of the right materials. A certain type of door, to take a specific case, costs $2.00 when built of the best materials. Made from the cheapest possible substitutes, it will cost $1.00. (These are quite accurate figures and not the guesswork that the round numbers seem to imply.) Apparently the cheap door has cut the cost in half, but what have we lost?

To begin with, it takes twice (often three or four times) as long to build with cheap lumber. Of course our stagehands are not paid except in fun, but their time is valuable and the fun of driving nails in boards that split and splinter may be overrated. Second, our door is sure to be warped and will never either swing properly or look well. Third, we are almost certain to spoil some of our inferior materials while working with them. Fourth, the cheap door will rarely outlast three plays, so its cost per play is $33\frac{1}{3}$¢. The good door will stand almost any sort of treatment for at least twenty plays, bringing its cost down to 10¢ per play. Lastly, when the good door finally falls apart it still has a very real salvage value, while the only thing worth saving from the poor door will be the latch.

The Plane Principle. Almost all scenery is made from a combination of lumber and some sort of fabric, usually canvas. Although wood can be carved and cloth can be draped or tailored, both these materials lend themselves more readily to flat surfaces than to curved and irregular ones. For this reason it is well to conceive and build every possible scene-unit as a plane or a simple arrangement of planes (e. g. a door-frame).

Sometimes the planes are disguised by applied ornament. (See the fireplace on p. 91.) Sometimes methods have been devised that make the construction of particular three-dimensional objects (e. g. tree trunks and Roman arches) surprisingly easy. Nevertheless the plane rule is fundamental and if not followed will cause trouble in the most unexpected places. The warning "Curve—Danger" should be posted above every scene designer's work table.

Typical Scene-Units

We are now ready to examine the different types of scene-units that have been evolved and to see how they are used to simulate the various architectural and natural elements that we may expect to encounter.

The flat is the fundamental scene-unit and is the one from which the walls of most sets are built. In its simplest form it is a rectangular framework of light wood covered with canvas (p. 73). Since wide flats are difficult to build and awkward to handle, most walls are made of two or three flats hinged together. Many flats have openings built into them (p. 81) to take doorframes, windows, etc. Following the unit principle, such accessories are never made as an integral part of the flat.

A number of other scenic elements are really flats masquerading under special names. Stage ceilings (p. 141) are large flats hung overhead. The simpler forms of stage doors ("F" p. 87) are built like small flats. A whole class of scene-units, called **cut-outs** because of their irregular edges, is used to imitate rock forms, bushes, distant mountains, etc. (p. 99). Many cut-outs are merely plain flats, with edges of the required shape attached, and even the most elaborate varieties are built on the principles employed in flat construction.

The flat is also the basis of a number of three-dimensional forms. The fireplace on p. 91, for instance, is really two small flats disguised by the application of molding and other ornaments.

Draperies of some opaque material, like cotton flannel or cotton velvet, can often be substituted for flats. When used as walls they are hung from **battens** made of wood or pipe. These battens may be either suspended from the grid or supported on uprights standing on the stage floor.

Whole scenes made of draperies are called **cyclorama sets.** Ceilings are not suited to such sets, so **borders** are used instead. These are valances hung overhead to mask the flies (p. 21). They are usually of the same material as the main drapes and are hung in folds.

While it is possible for actors to enter between any two draperies, doors and other built units lend so much to the realism of the cyclorama set that they should be added wherever possible. "A" p. 15, shows the back view of a window placed between two drapes. Notice that the cloth is thumbtacked to the back of the frame and that the window is raised on stilts and provided with a skirt to mask the space under it.

Flats combine well with cyclorama sets. "B" p. 15, shows the front view of a door flat, doorframe and door so used.

Natural forms are easily represented on stage. The cut-out type of flat serves for most cases where a lack of depth will not be noticeable. When trees are called for, the trunk and foliage are made separately. The trunks may be cut-outs although they are not difficult to build in the round (p. 99). One type of foliage is made from a flat hung on its side overhead and decorated with a fringe of canvas leaves. A more orthodox variety of **foliage border** is a flat piece of canvas cut to represent branches and suspended from a batten.

If the stage is not equipped with a permanent sky, there are several excellent substitutes. One is the **drop,** a large piece of canvas with battens at top and bottom. Any sort of scene may be painted on a drop, but for sky purposes it is well to forego clouds and stick to an even coat of blue. A sky viewed through a window may be merely a piece of blue muslin tacked on the back of the sash ; or a flat, painted blue, can be stood behind the window.

Steps and platforms are among the most useful scene-units. If they are kept simple in form they are also among the easiest to build, but irregularities make them very difficult. I recall one rock used in *Peer Gynt.* It was only 10′ 0″ x 4′ 0″ x 3′ 0″ (read "ten by four by three") but it was so complicated that I never succeeded in making a satisfactory working drawing of it. Instead I had to fall back on cut-and-try carpentry that took three of us the better part of a week. The result

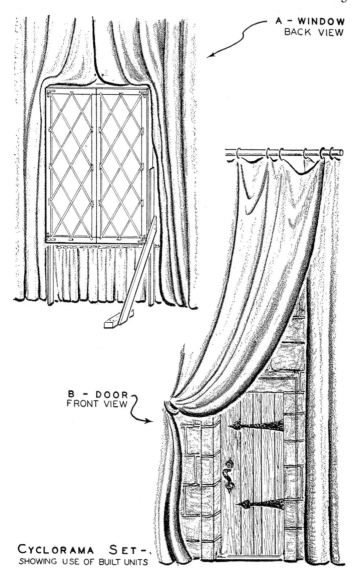

A – WINDOW
BACK VIEW

B – DOOR
FRONT VIEW

CYCLORAMA SET–
SHOWING USE OF BUILT UNITS

justified the trouble, but unless you have plenty of spare time, keep your steps and platforms simple.

Not all irregularities are equally serious. **Ramps,** for instance, which are sloping platforms, present few difficulties. Also note the oblique platforms used in the sets on p. 33.

Other Classifications

Often it is convenient to designate scenery by its use rather than by its structure. Thus we may speak of the **wall** of a stage room without regard to whether the wall is to be made of flats or drapes or a combination of both. Similarly, scenery placed behind an opening in the main set is called a **backing.** Backings may be anything from a blue sky-flat outside a window to the completely equipped dining room seen through a doorway in the Broadway production of *First Lady.*

A piece of scenery placed at the side of the stage to mask the wings is called a **wing.** Most wings are cut-outs, but plain flats, drapes, and three-dimensional forms are fairly common.

A **ground-row** is a horizontal unit placed upstage to disguise the line between sky and stage floor ("B" p. 33). Often they hide lighting instruments as well and provide a screen behind which actors can crawl from one side of the stage to the other without being seen. Three-dimensional ground-rows sometimes occur, but the vast majority are cut-outs.

Any piece of scenery used to simulate the third dimension is called a **thickness-piece** or simply a **thickness.** The little flats on each side of the opening in the stone wall of "A" p. 33 are examples. If this set were for a theater with a balcony it would need thicknesses for the top of the wall as well. The depth of a window or doorframe may also be spoken of as a thickness.

Stock Scenery

The secret of economical play production lies in accumulating a stock of all kinds of scene-units. These can then be assembled in any manner desired, like the parts of a child's construction set. Grouped in one way they form a kitchen; taken apart and rearranged they serve as a throne room. This inter-changeability may be disguised by paint, but structurally it is fundamental.

With such a stock of scenery it is possible to make sets as simple or as elaborate as you wish. My workshop group assembles and paints its sets in two or three evenings. The major productions use the same units but the scenes often require a month's work, due to their greater complexity and finish of detail.

A stock of scenery should be built up, rather than built. Except in rare instances, the amateur seldom constructs more than three or four new units for any one production. The secret lies in making these *standard,* so that they will fit in with the units that are already on hand and also with those planned for the future.

Flat Height. Scenery walls are higher than ordinary walls. A teaser less than 10′ 0″ or 10′ 6″ from the stage seems to be pressing down on the actors' heads. As the set must extend 1′ 0″ or 2′ 0″ above the teaser, this gives us 12′ 0″ as a minimum flat height except for very cramped stages. Now it so happens that the difficulty of building and handling flats increases rapidly after the 12′ 0″ height is passed, which means that this is not only a practical minimum but a practical maximum as well. Fortunately this causes no complication. I have standardized on 12′ 0″ flats for eight years and used them for every scene that came along. Sometimes I increased their apparent height by placing them on platforms or adding cornices. Sometimes I laid them on their sides for low walls. Occasionally I had to build a special flat, but on the whole they have served for every type of play from *Anna Christie* to *Julius Caesar.*

In auditoriums with high balconies, it may be necessary to raise the normal teaser height to 12′ 6″ to give a good view of the back wall. Where this is the case, the standard flat height must be 14′ 0″.

Flat widths run from 1′ 0″ to 5′ 9″. For widths less than 1′ 0″ a plain board may be substituted. Although the 5′ 9″ limit sounds arbitrary, it is merely a definite way of saying "a little less than six feet." Flats wider than 5′ 9″ are hard to store and handle. They cannot be covered with a single 72″ width of canvas, since shrinkage must be allowed for. They require extra framework. If these reasons seem insufficient, try building a few 8′ 0″ and 10′ 0″ flats and see how much trouble they cause.

Twenty-four flats will take care of most plays. My own stock contains forty-five, which is enough for even such a multi-scene production as *The Women*.

At this point the reader will want to know how to divide his flats among the various widths from 1′ 0″ to 5′ 9″. This is like the famous problem of how to propose. Many people worry about it, but in the end it answers itself. The dimensions given on p. 10 will provide helpful suggestions, but the simplest procedure is to build whatever flats you need for your first production and then try to use them in your second. You may have to add a few more, but these will enlarge your stock, and after the third or fourth production flat building practically stops.

Openings in Flats. For an ordinary door an opening 3′ 0″ wide and 7′ 0″ high should be provided. I have four flats with openings this size. One of these flats is 4′ 0″ wide and fits in many tight corners. The other three are 5′ 9″. One of them has the opening exactly in the center. In one of the others the opening is 1′ 0″ from the right-hand edge of the flat; in the third it is 1′ 0″ from the left-hand edge. I also have three 5′ 9″ flats with openings 4′ 4″ wide and 9′ 6″ high.

These flats may also be used for windows, bookcases, fireplaces, etc., by covering any unwanted part of the opening with canvas ("D" p. 81). This process is called **plugging**. It makes special flats for windows, etc., unnecessary.

Stock Drapery Units. As all the drapery units in a cyclorama set are the same height, and as the width of a drapery is adjustable, only one size unit is needed. For prosceniums less than 24′ 0″ in width, drapes 6′ 0″ wide are excellent. These may also be used on larger stages, but here 9′ 0″ drapes are more convenient. Units wider than 9′ 0″ should never be purchased. The "Scenic Companies" that equip schools usually make the mistake of supplying cycloramas with back walls consisting of two wide units. This handicaps the scene designer, as it forces him to put all upstage openings in the center. A wall made of narrow drapes will hang as one piece, yet openings may be placed anywhere.

As they are to be used with borders rather than ceilings, drapes should be taller than flats. Heights of 18' 0" or more are not uncommon on large stages, while 14' 0" is a practical minimum.

Ceiling. One ceiling will serve for all scenes. It should be 1' 0" or 2' 0" wider than the widest set we expect to use. In depth the ceiling may be about 1' 0" less than the depth of our deepest set since it is always hung at least 2' 0" upstage of the teaser to leave room for the lighting apparatus.

Stock Doors, Windows, etc. The openings in single doorframes should be 6' 8" high and 2' 8" wide. This is the usual architectural practice and has been found to work well on stage. The doors themselves (if they are to open offstage) overlap the frame and so must be 2' 9½" wide. The overlap at the top is compensated for by the necessity of leaving clearance at the bottom. This makes the doors 6' 8" high like the openings.

A good size for double-doorframes is 6' 8" x 4' 0". This takes two 6' 8" x 2' ¾" doors.

Single doors made to open onstage hang inside the frame and are only 6' 7" high and 2' 7¾" wide to allow for clearance.

Special window frames are unnecessary since doorframes can be converted to this purpose. The same thing is true of bookcases.

Stock Stairs. The horizontal part of each step is known as the **tread.** The vertical face is called the **riser.** With rare exceptions stage steps should be standardized with 10" treads and 7" risers. I have never tried to standardize stairs as to width and number of steps. Usually it is easier to plan scenes for whatever stairs are on hand, and then build others if the design demands them.

Stock Platforms. Platform heights are generally figured in terms of steps. A platform two steps high is 14", one three steps high is 21″, etc. As platform legs are interchangeable, and are 1″ less than the height of the platform, this means that the stock leg sizes are 13″ (2 × 7″ — 1″), 20″ (3 × 7″ — 1″), etc. Legs are so easy to make that only stock sizes are worth storing.

Most platform tops are rectangular, but a few oblique shapes are desirable for exterior scenes. During one period of three years I used platforms in half my sets and found that five rectangular and two oblique tops would meet all my needs. Two of the rectangular tops were 4′ 0″ x 10′ 0″, two were 5′ 0″ x 7′ 0″ and the fifth was 2′ 0″ x 7′ 0″. The oblique tops were 7′ 0″ long. One short side was 4′ 0″ and the other was 1′ 0″. The fourth side ran diagonally between the ends of the short sides. When fitted together along their diagonals they made up a 5′ 0″ x 7′ 0″ rectangle. Sets "B" and "C" p. 33 are examples of the many ways in which this set of platform tops can be used.

Economy Settings

The suggestions that follow show what can be done to reduce to a minimum the cost and effort required for scene building, without sacrificing the possibilities for future growth.

Minimum Sets. Even where first cost is the controlling factor and we have no equipment to start with, it is false economy to skimp on the quality of our materials. Good scene-units are an investment, and may be used over and over again. Poor units are merely an expense.

We can, however, cut down on the quantity of our scenery. Page 21 shows one scheme for doing this. The back wall of the stage house is made to serve as the back wall of the set by decorating it with a fireplace, a pair of dummy windows, and a picture. The backs of the windows are covered with blue material for day scenes, or black material for night scenes. Sash curtains and window draperies keep the artificiality of this device from being too obvious.

The side walls are draperies of cotton flannel. They are hung from wooden battens which are supported by uprights from

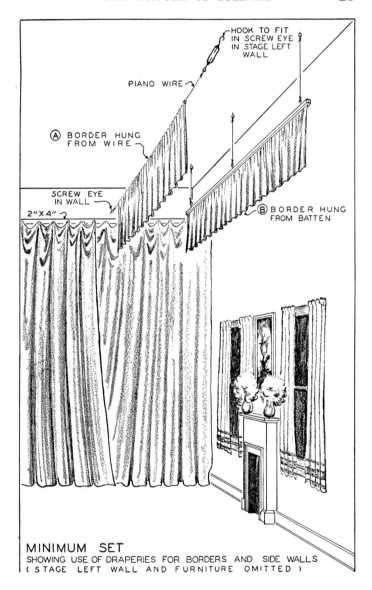

HOOK TO FIT
IN SCREW EYE
IN STAGE LEFT
WALL

PIANO WIRE

(A) BORDER HUNG
FROM WIRE

SCREW EYE
IN WALL

2"X 4"

(B) BORDER HUNG
FROM BATTEN

MINIMUM SET
SHOWING USE OF DRAPERIES FOR BORDERS AND SIDE WALLS
(STAGE LEFT WALL AND FURNITURE OMITTED)

the floor. Entrances and exits are made where two drapes come together, although doors like the one shown on p. 15 may be added if desired.

If the ceiling of the stage house is low, it will serve as the ceiling of the set, but if it is high, borders must be used. These may be supported by battens hung from screw eyes in the ceiling, or merely strung on piano wire run between screw eyes in the sides of the stage and kept taut with a **turnbuckle.** If the latter method is used, make sure the screw eyes are strong and firmly imbedded in the wall, as the strain on them is very great.

A minimum exterior set is shown at "A" p. 33. This calls for a flat with a door in it, two flats laid on their sides to form a stone wall, a ground-row (also made from a flat), a foliage border, and two tree trunks. The tree trunks serve as wings. They may be made from drapes hung from curved pieces of wood. The additional wings and the backing shown in the sketch may be omitted where extreme economy is necessary.

These sets are far from masterpieces, but the material for them can be had for $10.00 or $20.00. Furthermore, the units from which they are made serve as a nucleus that can be added to until a whole stock of scenery is built up.

Convertible Sets. Where an investment of as much as $100.00 can be made, it is possible to construct a convertible set that reduces the cost and effort of future scene building to almost zero. The drawings on p. 10 show the units that make up such a set. (A ceiling should be added. See the dotted line on "B" p. 31.) By rearranging these units, hundreds of different scenes can be made. Those on p. 31 serve as examples. The numbers indicate how the flats fit into each scene. Compare these two pages of drawings carefully. They probably make the basic principles of scenery clearer than anything I could write.

With a convertible set only occasional items such as the ticket window and the railings in "C" will need to be built **special.** Frequently even these can be kept, and will increase the future adaptability of the set. If the walls are painted a neutral tone, the need for further painting can be eliminated. Of course, such a set has its limitations. Plays like *L'Aiglon* and *Yellow Jack* are beyond its reach. On the other hand, it will meet all the needs of a not-too-ambitious group that is willing to arrange its season with its scenic equipment in mind.

A Three Year Plan. No matter how closely a group must watch the pennies, it can still build up a satisfactory stock of scenery by adding a few units each production. Starting with a minimum set, or a drapery-cyclorama, the first season can be spent in building doors, windows, and a few flats. These flats should be made in such widths that they can later be used to form a convertible set. During the second season enough flats can be built to finish the convertible set. If a ceiling is included so much the better, but if not, borders may still be substituted. The third season should add still more flats, and perhaps a few steps, platforms, and other useful items. With these it will be possible to take the flats apart, and rearrange and repaint them for each show. Even with a budget as small as $10.00 a play, an active group should be able to accumulate a complete stock of scenery in three years.

CHAPTER IV

PRACTICAL SCENE DESIGN

Much has been written on the esthetic side of scene design. We are told that the set should not obtrude but should form a background for the action; that the locale and the time should be conveyed by the setting; and that the scenery should conform to the mood and style of the play. This is all true, but our informants either fail to explain, or never knew, that the practical side of scene design is as important as the esthetic. In some respects it is more so.

From one point of view the most interesting aspect of design lies in the fact that it controls both the cost and the effort required to make scenery. There is an enormous difference between the simplest possible set that will meet the requirements of a given play and the most elaborate one that could be justified. Before starting to work, the designer should make up his mind just how much the production is worth to his group in time and money, and govern himself accordingly.

Drawings

One of the chief differences between the expert scene builder and the novice is that the expert makes drawings of the things he intends to build, while the novice does not. Actually the beginner needs drawings far more than the experienced worker, since the latter already carries a great deal of information in his head.

This does *not* mean that drawings need to be either elaborate or beautiful. They merely represent *a working out on paper of the thing to be done*. A mistake made with a pencil can be corrected with an eraser. A mistake made with a saw takes a lot of the fun out of scene building.

Most of the cuts in this book are not working drawings but illustrations. There is a great difference. Illustrations are intended to be understood at a glance by anyone. That is why I have shown the third dimension in so many of them. Working drawings, on the other hand, are simplified and conventionalized, and while these conventions are easy to learn, one must be familiar with them if one is to read such drawings easily. College courses in stagecraft usually provide formal instruction in drafting. This is necessary because the working conditions in most college theaters require scenery to be built from blueprints and with a minimum of verbal directions. Furthermore, students can learn almost as much about the structure of an object by making a careful drawing of it as they could by actually building it. Skill in drafting is valuable, but by no means essential. The important point is that many of the same problems that arise in building a scene, or a scene-unit, also come up while a drawing is being made. Students learn to recognize these problems, and must solve them in order to complete their drawings. In this way they learn more with less work.

The drawings used in school and community theater work are much less elaborate. In fact most of them are as simple and crude as the sketches on p. 43. Sometimes, as in "C," they scarcely represent the object at all, but are merely skeleton diagrams on which the dimensions can be indicated. In work of this sort the drawings are made chiefly for the designer's own benefit. If his drawings are clear to him, that is sufficient. When necessary, he can explain them to his co-workers. As long as the drawing is complete enough and accurate enough for the designer to be sure he understands exactly how the item sketched is to be built, anything more is superfluous. Anything less is borrowing trouble at interest.

Drawing Equipment. A lead pencil, scratch paper, and an eraser will meet most of our requirements, though a ruler (preferably of the transparent type) is very useful. Some of

our drawings, however, must be made to scale and for them
we will save time if we add the following equipment:

Drawing board	— 18″ x 24″ or larger.
T-square	— 24″ or longer.
30°–60° triangle	— 6″.
45° triangle	— 10″.
Architect's scale	— 12″.
Compass	— for drawing curves.
Drawing pencils	— 2H grade.
Sandpaper block	— for sharpening the pencils.
Tracing paper	— on which the drawings are made.
Bristol board	— to be placed under the paper to give a hard, white surface to draw on.
Thumbtacks	— to hold the paper to the board.

This outfit will cost about $4.00. With a little practice, even
the novice can produce accurate drawings almost as quickly
as he can turn out the roughest free-hand sketch, the only difference being the time required to make the necessary measurements. Nothing develops one's constructive imagination so
much as mechanical drawing. It is easy. Try it. Drafting supplies are sold at most blueprint shops and the salesman can
show you how to use them. Probably the only instrument that
will require explanation is the scale. That is hard to describe
in words but simple enough to understand from a demonstra-
tion. A scale is a very useful device since it enables us to
measure a line on a drawing directly in feet and inches.

If colored sketches are to be made, water color is the best
medium, although colored pencils or even wax crayon will do.
The shop that supplies the pigments can also advise as to
brushes, paper, etc. For scene design purposes, cheap paints
are as good as the best.

Floor Plans. The most important of all working drawings
is the floor plan of the set. This should be made to a scale of
½″ = 1′ 0″, and must be carefully and accurately drawn so
that the exact size of each object will be represented. "B"
p. 31 is a good example of a floor plan except that its small
size made it impossible to include any dimensions. Note that

a line is drawn separating each two flats. An X on the onstage end of the line means that the flats hinge on the front. The little wiggles on the offstage ends of the other lines indicate that the adjoining flats are to be lashed together (p. 127). These symbols, and others that the designer can add himself, are very handy. All furniture is drawn to scale.

Two reference lines, from which measurements can be made, should be shown on the plan. One of these, called the **tormentor-line,** is drawn between the tormentors. The other, which is in the middle of the stage and perpendicular to the footlights, is the **center-line.** These lines should be dotted to avoid any confusion with the lines of the set itself.

Elevations. Usually the scene builder actually works from an **elevation,** in which each unit is shown directly from the front without any attempt to indicate perspective. "A" and "B" on p. 43 are examples. Side and rear elevations are also employed. The latter are particularly valuable, as they usually show the more important structural details. College courses in stagecraft generally require rear elevations of all scene-units. In community and school theaters, however, it is often simpler to sketch a front elevation and indicate any unusual construction features by dotted lines.

The designer should make a separate elevation of each wall of the set showing the location of all openings and of any built-on decorations. If produced for college classes, these drawings should be carefully made and should show all details. School and community theaters need only the roughest sort of sketches in most cases, but all dimensions must be given.

Sections. Sometimes construction details are shown best by drawing them as if the object had been cut through with a knife. Examples of this will be found at "E" p. 83, "E" p. 87 and "C" p. 99. This sort of drawing is called a **section.** Usually the parts that seem to have been cut are shaded with diagonal lines to distinguish them from the parts shown in the background. The examples mentioned all illustrate this.

Sketches. A colored sketch, showing the set as it will look from the audience, is a great help in planning the effect to be produced. Anyone can draw well enough to make a useful sketch. As a matter of fact, inability to draw is almost a characteristic of New York theatrical designers. (I know one who gets his perspective backward!)

Most beginners, whether they draw well or badly, choose a viewpoint that is too high. This brings out the construction, which is why I have done the same thing in the illustrations on pp. 31 and 33, but it falsifies the effect of the scene. The proper viewpoint is 40' 0" or 50' 0" from the tormentor-line and 4' 0" or 5' 0" above the stage floor.

Models for interior sets are easily made. A long strip of cardboard, with the doors and windows drawn on it, represents the walls and may easily be bent to the shape of the floor plan. If a model is to have any value, it *must* be made to scale, preferably $\frac{1}{2}" = 1'\,0"$. A model that is not to scale is misleading and certain to cause trouble.

In designing a set that is to contain a number of stock platforms, we can save time by making a special kind of model. This consists of small pieces of $\frac{1}{4}"$ wallboard the shape of the platforms. The size should be figured at $\frac{1}{2}"$ to the foot. Thus a $2" \times 5"$ rectangle represents a $4'\,0" \times 10'\,0"$ platform and the $\frac{1}{4}"$ thickness of the board is near enough to scale to stand for $7"$, the height of one step. Several such pieces should be provided for each platform so that, by piling them on top of one another, model platforms of different heights can be made. With such a model we can set up an arrangement in five minutes and change it at will. Steps need not be represented, since they can be kept in mind.

Design and the Director

To the audience a set is merely a background, but actually its chief purpose is to facilitate the action of the play: doors are located to permit effective entrances and exits, steps and platforms placed to support interesting groupings, and furniture arranged to allow the actors to assume a wide variety of easy, natural positions. These matters are fundamentally problems for the director, but since they affect and often control the form of the set, the designer should be familiar with them.

Realism. If we wish to make our scenery convincing, we must consider how our stage room would fit into a real house. The arrangement of furniture is also important in this connection. It is amazing how even the best commercial designers have ignored this point. Study the plan in the back of almost any printed play and observe how little the furniture has to do with the set. In at least half the scenes we find dreary repetitions of the "sofa and chair on one side—table and two chairs on the other" formula. Here is one situation in which the amateur can often outdo the professional.

The difficulty of providing a natural furniture arrangement is caused by several factors. One is the limited wall space provided by the three-walled stage room. Another depends on the need for keeping the faces of the actors visible. It is rarely wise to turn a chair more than 90° away from the audience, or to mask a seat or a door by placing furniture downstage of it. One idea that may prove helpful is to have a fireplace in a side wall with a sofa at right angles to it facing the footlights. Another is to use a coffee table or other low, backless piece of furniture like a hassock or even a box. These do not hide any action that takes place behind them, may serve as either chairs or tables, and may be sat on from any angle.

Location of Scene Elements. Doors used for important entrances should be in the back wall if possible. The door in the barrack-room scene in *Brother Rat* furnishes a good example, since it is used for several dramatic entrances while the exits are comparatively weak. When an exit is the controlling factor, as in *A Doll's House,* the door should be in a side wall. If the same door must be used for both important exits and entrances, as in *You Can't Take It with You,* it should also be in a side wall, for it is easy to make a good entrance from the side but very difficult to make a good exit upstage.

Most stage doors swing offstage because doors which swing onstage are hard to build. Doors in the side walls should have their hinges on the upstage edge. A door in the middle of the back wall may hinge on either edge, but if placed to one side it usually hinges on the edge away from the center of the stage.

These rules sound arbitrary, but I can think of only two exceptions. One is where a character hides behind an open door. Here the door must swing onstage. The other applies to mystery plays, where a creepy effect may be obtained by having doors in the side walls swing onstage and hinging them on the downstage edge. This builds up every entrance, since the audience sees the door move and wonders what sort of creature will appear.

Windows used for exits or entrances are treated as doors. When a character is to look in through a window, it must be in the back wall. If the character will have to describe off stage action, supposedly seen through a window, the window should be in a side wall, preferably as far downstage as possible.

Fireplaces used against a side wall motivate many cross-stage movements and interesting groupings. Fireplaces in a back wall are of little value except as decoration, because actors placed before them tend to have their backs to the audience.

Furniture arrangement should be planned so that the grouping and movements of the actors will be natural and effective. The floor plan at "B" p. 31 was designed by David McIntosh and William J. McMullin for the main scene of *First Lady*. The furniture is a little crowded, as this set was originally used on a 30′ 0″ stage and has been drawn only 26′ 0″ wide. Otherwise it supplies an almost perfect example of furniture placement. It would be easy to think of this as part of a real room, yet no seat is turned away from the audience and no upstage piece (except unimportant tables) is masked. The rectangle below the love seat up-left represents a low coffee table. Notice also that we have two main furniture groups, one down-right and one up-left. The up-left group is particularly interesting, since it may be thought of as the love seat alone, or (by properly placing the actors) may be extended to include the chairs in the center and the one down-left as well. The light chairs are especially adaptable since they can be moved during the action to permit new groupings. The tea scene in Act III, for instance, may be played center by bringing on a butler's tray and arranging the small chairs around it.

The office set at "A," while equally realistic, is less satis-

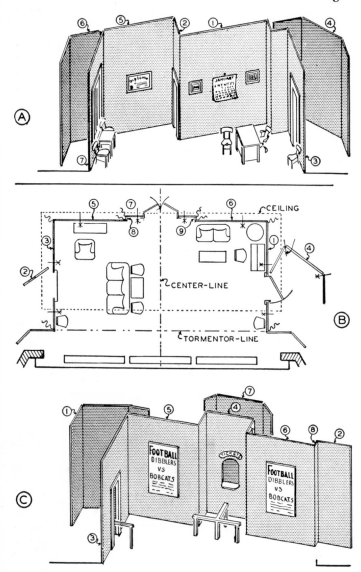

factory. Two main furniture groups are provided, but they are both downstage and the usefulness of the one on stage right is decidedly limited. The plan might be improved by placing a bench against the wall marked "5," if this could be done without blocking the doorway. Another improvement would be to reverse the set entirely so that the desk comes on stage right. The desk will obviously be the focal point for the important scenes, and for some obscure—but very real—psychological reason stage right is dramatically stronger than stage left.

Platform arrangement has been described as "deciding where the actors are to stand and then building platforms under them." This is illustrated by the scene at "B" p. 33, which was designed for *High Tor*. The tall platform up-right serves for the Indian's prayer. Downstage of it are diagonal steps on which Van and Lise can sit during their first scene. The platforms at the back provide a low point behind which the steam shovel can hang without being hidden, and they also furnish a path for the Dutchmen to cross in silhouette. All important scenes should be worked out in this way. Minor scenes can be left for rehearsal.

In such sets we must make sure that the actors can walk easily from any part of the set to any other part. It is also well to arrange matters so that the natural movements are diagonal rather than cross-stage or up and down.

The use of steps and platforms in interior scenes is simpler than in exteriors, but it is no less effective. Between 40% and 50% of all interiors can employ at least one or two platforms and steps to match. These units are so cheap and easy to build, and add so much to the dramatic possibilities of the set, that they should be included in the design wherever the nature of the scene permits.

One word of caution may be necessary. A platform in front of a door must be duplicated by another offstage; otherwise the actor in making an exit will step off into space. Dress rehearsal is a little late to discover this. Such offstage platforms are called **getaway** platforms, and we also speak of getaway stairs.

The effect of an exterior set depends in no small measure on how it is painted. "B" is a far better set than "A," yet it loses

BACKING

Ⓐ

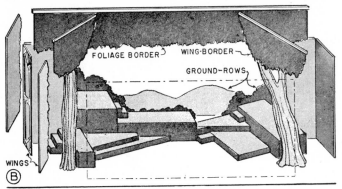

FOLIAGE BORDER   WING-BORDER

GROUND-ROWS

WINGS

Ⓑ

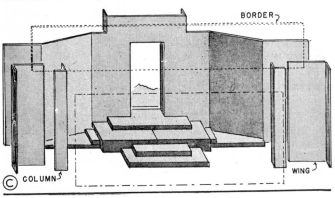

BORDER

COLUMN   WING

Ⓒ

much of its effectiveness because the paint detail is not shown. This does not mean that every exterior should be elaborately painted. The platforms in "B," for instance, should be a greenish brown monotone and will depend on the lights for their interest. In general, the simpler the lighting is, the more complicated the painting must be and *vice versa.*

The matter of set **dressing** should also be considered. Dressing includes all the small decorations on the stage. The vines on the stage right wall in "A" p. 33 are one example, and the calendar and pictures on the walls in "A" p. 31 form another. The importance of dressing is being acknowledged in the motion pictures by placing the set-dresser's name on the program. Generally speaking the more dressing a set has the better, although of course there are many cases such as "C" p. 33 where any dressing at all would be ridiculous.

Technical Considerations

An effective picture is only a small part of a usable scene design. The work of men like Bakst and Gordon Craig is proof of this. On paper their drawings are magnificent, but the problems of translating them to the stage are not only unsolved, they are apparently not even considered. Since we wish to design scenery for the theater and not for picture books, we must at least know what these problems are.

The Stage. Most amateurs design for a particular stage, and it is important to have this stage in mind when planning a set. I worked for five years on a stage the back wall of which was only 14' 0" from the proscenium, and this dimension governed everything I did. My present stage has a beam 16' 0" above the center of the floor. Usually this is a serious liability; occasionally it is an asset. In either case, it has a direct effect on the scenery I build. Measured drawings of the stage, made to a scale of $\frac{1}{2}'' = 1'\,0''$, are of immense value in planning scenery.

The Stock on Hand. Stock scene-units materially reduce the cost and effort of scene building and a good designer will utilize his stock as far as possible. A list of stock flats and platform tops, or better still a complete inventory of all stored scenery, should lie at the designer's elbow while he works. The trouble of making such a list will be repaid twice over even for one production.

The materials and properties available can also profitably be kept in mind. At one time or another I have designed scenes to take advantage of the chance possession of such items as a circus chariot, a quantity of artificial wisteria, and the canvas from some second-hand drops.

Cost and Difficulty. It is hard to imagine such plays as *Lazarus Laughed* and *Cyrano de Bergerac* being staged either easily or cheaply, but if plays are selected with due regard for the scenery both the trouble and the expense of scene building are in the hands of the scene designer. Two opposite examples of this came up in my own productions last season. The script of *The Skull* calls for a simple cyclorama. We could have rigged ours in an hour. Instead we elected to build a Gothic chapel 24′ 0″ high, complete with stained glass windows and organ loft. That took six weeks of hard work. Shaw's *You Never Can Tell* requires a terrace and a living room. By placing the terrace outside an enormous window, we were able to combine these sets and save both time and money.

Similar considerations apply to details. A door that swings onstage costs four times as much as one that swings offstage; a casement window is simpler than a double-hung window; and a Roman arch is easier to build than a Gothic one. The cut-outs on p. 99 furnish a particularly good example of the relationship between design and difficulty. The ground-row at "D" can be made in half an hour. "E," because of its greater complications, will take half a day.

Construction Methods. If the designer does not understand how scenery is built, he should work with someone who does. A set is emphatically not a picture on paper, but a structure of wood, and canvas, and hardware. If the designer does not know how every item in the set is to be made, he is only designing trouble for the building crew.

Scene Shifts. When a play calls for more than one scene, the shifts must be considered as well as the individual sets. In plays like *Dodsworth* and *Abe Lincoln in Illinois,* where the shift problem is particularly acute, it may be necessary to devise the shift plan before designing the scenery.

Even where the scene changes present no inherent difficulties, the designer often has an opportunity for simplification. In *First Lady,* for instance, the shifts are much easier if Act II, Sc. 1 is made small enough to fit inside the set used for the rest of the play. Another type of situation is very common on stages with low gridirons. Plays like *The Firebrand* and *Brother Rat* call for both interiors (presumably with a ceiling) and exteriors (presumably with foliage borders). Unfortunately, a low gridiron makes the shift from ceiling to borders almost impossible. One solution is to substitute beam-like borders for the ceiling. The point is that the problem belongs not to the scenes themselves but to the shifts, and must be solved before the sets are designed.

Two or more sets are not always harder to build than one. Audiences expect more finish in a single set, and there are other compensations. *Men in White,* for instance, requires seven different scenes. Since they are all laid in the same hospital, they can all be the same color. Advantage may be taken of this by planning a convertible set that can be rearranged to serve for the seven scenes. If he will diagnose his problem in this manner, the designer can often turn a difficult play into an easy one.

Sight-lines

Before a set is built, the designer should know how much of the stage will be visible from the audience. The ordinary interior scene causes little difficulty in this regard. With exteriors, however, the necessity of masking the top and sides of the stage house may determine the basic design of the set. The set at "C" p. 33, which represents the type of conventional background used with Greek tragedy, illustrates this. If our stage is equipped with a dome, the set need only consist of the platforms, the back wall and the two square columns. But if our background is restricted to a drop or a plastered back wall, it is obvious that wings will be needed to hide the side walls of the stage and that the flies will have to be masked by a border. The wings can be pairs of flats painted to match the main set, but the border offers several possibilities. We might use a strip of blue cloth and hope that the audience will accept it as part of the sky. We might use black cloth and pretend it is part of the inner proscenium. We might even substitute tree trunks for the columns as an excuse for employing a foliage border. None of these devices is satisfactory for this type of scene. A fourth method, shown in the illustration, is to convert the columns into a sort of inner-inner proscenium by the use of a border with a thickness-piece running upstage from its lower edge. This is far from Greek, but it has an appropriately formal quality and does wonders for the overhead masking.

Horizontal sight-lines are worked out by placing a piece of tracing paper, with the essential details of the set drawn on it, over a plan showing the stage and the first few rows of the auditorium. For this purpose accurate scaling is all-important.

Our first problem is to discover how much of the scene will be visible to all the members of the audience. To do this we start from the seats in the worst possible positions on each side of the auditorium. In some cases these will be the seats on the ends of the first row ("a" and "a' " in "A" p. 39) ; in others, those on the ends of the first full-length row ("b" and "b' "). In the set shown, two pairs of sight-lines are drawn, one ("c" and "c' ") just missing the tormentors and one ("d" and "d' ") just missing the edges of the door opening. The first pair is usually all that is needed, but some scenes may require three or more sets. The director must arrange the action of the play so that no important scene takes place outside these sight-lines. In the diagram the visible area is shaded to make the situation clear. In practice, such shading is unnecessary

Diagram "B" shows how the sizes and locations of the **masking pieces** are determined. Lines are drawn from the end seats of the first row so as just to miss the onstage edges of the tormentors, wing pieces, etc. Note that in this diagram, the people sitting on the right-hand end of the first rows near "a'" can see into the stage right wings ("e," "f," and "g"). This has been corrected on stage left by extending the ground-row "h" and the back wall "k," making the wing larger ("j"), and adding a thickness-piece 1′ 6″ wide to the tormentor ("i"). Such **tormentor-thicknesses** are made like narrow flats and are the full height of the inner proscenium opening. In all the drawings on this plate the stage is supposed to be equipped with a blue-plastered back wall which serves as a sky. If a drop is used it must be drawn in to scale.

If we draw lines touching the offstage edges of the columns and the onstage edges of the tormentors, as in diagram "C," and project these lines into the auditorium, we get another type of sight-line test. Take the line marked "m," for example. The members of the audience sitting below this line (in the diagram) could see into the stage right wings if it were not for the wing piece "l." In this case, line "m" tells us that the wing must be moved farther onstage if it is to be completely effective. Sight-line "n" shows that the stage left wing is properly placed.

Vertical Sight-lines. The sight-lines that cause the greatest difficulty are not those on the stage floor, but those in the air. The more important of these are worked out on a vertical section showing the auditorium and the stage. (See diagram "E," which is intended merely as an illustration of sight-line problems and *not* as an example of good theater design.) The sight-line used to determine what part of the stage will be visible is shown at "u." It starts from the back row of the balcony ("t") at eye level (3′ 8″ from the floor) and passes just under the teaser. In this case, we learn that the head of an actor standing at "y" will be hidden unless the teaser is raised.

If the auditorium has no balcony, this sight-line is not important except for scenes with second floors as in *She Loves Me Not,* or with balconies as in *Romeo and Juliet.* In such cases, a sight-line is taken from the back row of the orchestra "v."

If we are compelled to raise the teaser it will cause masking difficulties, as can be seen from line "w." In "D" these difficulties are corrected by making the border "r" deeper and by

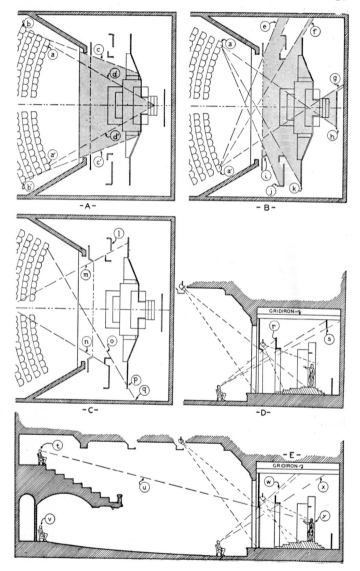

- A -

- B -

- C -

- D -

- E -

using a **teaser-thickness,** similar to the tormentor-thicknesses already described.

"D" also shows the use of a teaser-thickness to mask lighting instruments. Note in "E" that if the instruments are hung high enough to be out of sight-lines without such a thickness, the border would cast a shadow on the face of an actor standing at "y" and would have to be supplemented by additional lights hung behind the border.

Although teaser- and tormentor-thicknesses are very useful, they interfere with the adjustment of the inner proscenium, and this point should be considered before installing them.

Line "x" in "E" indicates that the upstage end of the grid-iron can be seen from the first few rows. This is corrected in "D" by hanging a second border at "s." The second border should be made inconspicuous by hanging it as high as possible, as there is no architectural excuse for its existence.

Some important sight-lines are not clearly shown either on the plan or on the section. Line "o" in diagram "C" is an instance. This touches the upstage edge of the column and, passing *over* the top of the back wall of the set at "p," strikes the side wall of the stage house at "q." This tells us that the upper part of the side wall will be visible from "q" to the back wall of the stage house, but it does not tell us the height of the visible area. The latter problem can be solved only on a special drawing or with the use of a model, so amateurs generally prefer to do a little inspired guessing. To mask the side wall in this particular case, a **wing-border,** made of a wide flat, can be hung against the wall in a position determined by actual trial. The other side of the stage must be masked in the same way. "B" p. 33 shows two foliage wing-borders used in different positions but with the same purpose.

Designing for Stock Units

A set that is to include platforms must be worked out with the available platforms in mind. The simplest way to do this is to use the special model described on p. 28. It is impossible to design the setting first and then try to fit stock platforms to it, unless we are prepared to build a number of specials. The same thing applies to doors, windows, trees, etc., but these present no difficulty since the number of possible combinations is limited.

When designing the walls of a set, however, the stock flats may almost be forgotten until the design is finished, because the flats can be assigned afterward. At first thought it seems impossible to take a random group of flats and make them fit a previously designed set, but in practice it is easy. We rarely have to change the width of a wall as much as an inch to be able to make our flats match it exactly. Nevertheless, we must keep in mind the number and size of our door flats. If there are only five such flats available they obviously cannot be used to form a set with a built-in bookcase, two windows and three doors.

Numbering. Time can be saved by assigning a number to each flat. It is desirable to have the numbers indicate the sizes of the flats. This may be done by giving flats from 2′ 0″ to 2′ 11″ numbers in the twenties, flats from 3′ 0″ to 3′ 11″ numbers in the thirties, and so on. Often it is possible to make the units figure equal the inches (e. g. a flat 4′ 4″ wide may be numbered "44"). This is not always practical as there may be two flats the same size (e. g. two 2′ 6″ flats must be numbered "25" and "26"). Also such cases as 1′ 10″ and 1′ 11″ have to be given numbers like "18" and "19." Numbers from "1" to "9" are arbitrarily assigned to door flats. As there are always several 5′ 9″ flats these are given numbers in the sixties. Under this system there will, of course, be many more numbers than there are flats.

The back of each flat should carry its number painted in black on a white ground (p. 73). If the numbers are repeated on the wooden uprights about 5′ 0″ from the floor, it will make the flat easier to find when it is stacked with others in a pile.

It is a good idea to have the flat list mimeographed or hectographed. If this is done, a copy can be used for each play and the flats checked off as they are assigned.

Assigning flats to the various walls of a set is easy at first because there is a large variety of flats from which to choose. As the work goes on it grows more difficult. For example, when we come to the last wall, all the flats may have been assigned except the following:

PLAIN FLATS

No. 24—2′ 5″	No. 33—3′ 3″	No. 49—4′ 10″
No. 27—2′ 7″	No. 40—4′ 0″	No. 50—5′ 0″

DOOR FLATS

No. 3—5′ 9″ wide, 4′ 4″ x 9′ 6″ opening
No. 7—4′ 0″ wide, 3′ 0″ x 7′ 0″ opening

Suppose our problem is to arrange some of these flats to make a wall 13′ 0″ wide, with a 3′ 0″ x 7′ 0″ opening, the center of which is to be 6′ 0″ from the left-hand edge of the wall. This situation is diagrammed at "a" in sketch "C" p. 43.

There are at least five arrangements of our flats which will produce a 13′ 0″ wall ("b" to "f"). As door flat No. 7 already

DESCRIPTION OF CUT ON OPPOSITE PAGE

This illustrates various types of rough sketches of the kind actually used in planning the construction of scenery, and which serve later as guides to the builder. Notice that everything is omitted except the essentials.

"A" is a free-hand sketch showing how a door flat with a large opening can be plugged for use behind a fireplace (p. 80). The dotted rectangle marks the permanent opening in the flat. The other dotted lines indicate the temporary framework used to outline the small opening. The large figure ("3") is the stock number of the flat.

"B" was drawn with a ruler. It shows how a stock door may be enlarged to fit a special doorframe. The upper rectangle is to be canvassed and the crack on the right of the sketch is to be covered with a stripper ("C" and "D" p. 77). These directions need not be noted on the drawing, since the building carpenter is either supposed to know them or can be told orally.

"C" shows the sort of crude diagram used in assigning flats. The top line "a" shows the width of the wall and the location of the center of the opening. The other figures represent various flat arrangements as they would appear on the floor plan of a set.

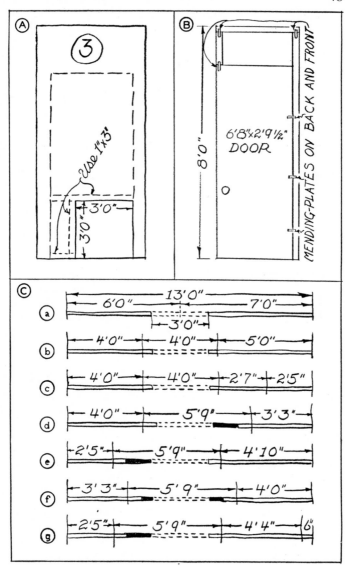

has an opening of the required size we can try that first ("b"). This matches our specifications exactly but is otherwise unsatisfactory because the flats will not fold (pp. 77 and 78). If, however, we substitute the two small flats for No. 40, as in "c," we get a result that will work, although using four flats for a 13′ 0″ wall is a clumsy expedient.

If we use flat No. 3 we must plug the 4′ 4″ x 9′ 6″ opening until only 3′ 0″ x 7′ 0″ is left. This smaller opening may be on the left side of the large one, on the right, or in the center. These three possibilities are shown at "d," "e," and "f" respectively. The heavy black marks indicate plugging.

Let us first examine "d." The combined widths of the three flats add up to 13′ 0″ (4′ 0″ + 5′ 9″ + 3′ 3″), so the over-all width is correct. Now the left-hand side of the opening in door flat No. 3 is 8½″ from the outside edge of the flat (5′ 9″ − 4′ 4″ = 17″, 17″ ÷ 2 = 8½″), and the center of the opening is to be 1′ 6″ from the sides (the opening is 3′ 0″ wide). Thus the center will come 2′ 2½″ (1′ 6″ + 8½″) from the left edge of the flat. But 4′ 0″ + 2′ 2½″ = 6′ 2½″, and this means that the opening will be 2½″ from where we want it. If we put the opening on the right, as in "e," we get: 4′ 10″ + 2′ 2½″ = 7′ ½″, a discrepancy of only ½″ which can be ignored. As this grouping is satisfactory the designer in actual practice would go no further. The reader, however, should examine the arrangement at "f." It is far from ideal, since the plugging of both sides of the large opening causes additional work, but it permits a wide latitude of small-opening placement and sometimes solves problems when nothing else will.

On rare occasions when it is impossible to make a wall of the desired size from the available stock, a flat may be enlarged by attaching a strip of wood to one edge. If, for example, we were compelled to substitute a 4′ 4″ flat for the 4′ 10″ flat shown in "f," we could still bring our wall to the right width by adding a 6″ board to the edge of the 4′ 4″ flat as indicated in "g."

If the calculations given above seem complicated, it is because they are difficult to explain and not because they are hard to perform. By working them out on paper for himself the reader can see that they are the simplest sort of arithmetic.

The process is worth mastering since stock flats cannot be used effectively without it.

Design Procedure

While the designer must keep all his problems more or less in his mind at once so that each can be gauged in the light of its effect on the others, the actual task of designing should be carried out in some sort of order. The exact order followed will depend on many things, but the method given here is typical.

Production Plan. To begin with, we need a general idea of our whole problem. Such questions as "How many scenes are there?"—"Can the same set be used for more than one scene?"—"Shall we use drapes or flats?"—"How much money can we spend?" are settled at this time. Most of these questions will answer themselves, but it never pays to overlook the obvious and a clear-cut approach will save trouble later.

Rough Floor Plan. In amateur work the director usually supplies at least the elements of the floor plan. He specifies the number of doors and their locations and gives a general idea of the amount of furniture required and how it is to be arranged. The designer then works these elements into a sketch of the floor plan, and has the director approve it, before going ahead.

Working Drawings. While there is no rule as to exactly what drawings the designer should prepare, it is well to make a floor plan of each set, an elevation of each wall, a color sketch of the set as a whole, and diagrams of any construction details that may prove troublesome.

The floor plan is generally made first so that it can serve as a base on which such matters as sight-lines and the assignment of flats can be worked out. Either the color sketch or the elevations may be made next, depending on the particular situation in hand. Details of construction are generally left until last, but if some feature of the set depends on a construction problem, the structural detail may have to be drawn before even the floor plan can be made.

The designer may omit any or all of these drawings but a set must be designed before it can be built. Somehow, some way, a decision has to be made as to the location of each board and the color of each brushful of paint. My experience has been that it is easier to design with a pencil than with a hammer.

CHAPTER V

TOOLS

Good tools are a great help on stage. It is impossible to expect much enthusiasm from a building crew that is asked to work with poor equipment. Carpenters, cabinetmakers and others who are familiar with tools in general, find difficulty in giving advice as to the tools needed on stage because they are not acquainted with the type of work involved. On this account I have listed practically every tool for which the scene builder may find use. The specifications given are, of course, not absolute and the reader who has had personal experience with tools may consider changes advisable. The prices quoted are intended to apply to the cheapest satisfactory grade. I have found it economical to purchase tools from the big chain stores such as Sears-Roebuck, Montgomery Ward, etc. Dime store tools are of poor quality, and tools sold in hardware stores are apt to be expensive.

Of the tools listed below only those marked ** are required for everyday work. Those marked * are necessary for carrying out certain special processes (e. g. a vise is needed for metal work) but the occasions demanding them are so rare that it is often as satisfactory to borrow as to own them. Tools marked †, while not strictly necessary, are so convenient and time-saving that they should certainly be included in the tool kit if funds permit.

Measuring and Marking Tools

Although great accuracy is rarely required in stagecraft, care in measuring and squaring is necessary for good work.

Rule ** (6′ 0″ folding type, 20¢ each) used for making measurements. In spite of the fact that all dimensions given in carpentrywork are expressed in feet and inches, the rules commonly sold are marked in consecutive inches. This requires constant mental arithmetic (e. g. 4′ 3″ must be converted to 51″ and *vice versa*). Rules marked in feet and inches are made, and sell for 45¢ each, but they are hard to find and if ordered from the factory must be bought in half-dozen lots.

Steel Square ** ($1.35 each) illustrated on p. 95. Whole books have been written on the uses of the steel square. Hardly anything can be built without one. The type with the marking painted in white is more expensive but convenient.

Try-Square † (6″ combination try and miter type, 60¢ each) used as a guide in marking wood for cutting (p. 69). The miter feature, which permits the square to be set at 45°, is valuable and should not be overlooked.

Sliding T-Bevel (6″, 40¢ each) like the try-square except that the blade can be set at any angle.

Plumb Bob (iron, 15¢ each) used to obtain a true vertical.

Carpenter's Level (18″, $1.25 each) a straight piece of wood containing two or more spirit levels. It is used to test the vertical and horizontal members of a structure.

Cutting Tools

As the tools listed below are for cutting, they should be kept sharp. Usually the sharpening requires more skill than the average amateur possesses and must be done by a professional.

Crosscut Saw ** (eight or nine teeth to the inch, 26″ or 28″ long, $2.50 each) for cutting wood or wallboard; often serves as a general purpose saw. If more than three or four people are to work at one time two crosscut saws will be necessary.

Ripsaw (five or six teeth to the inch, 26″ or 28″ long, $2.50 each). Sawing with the grain is called **ripping.** Crosscut saws are inefficient for this purpose and a ripsaw should be used if available.

Combination Saw * (consists of a handle and three interchangeable blades, 90¢ per set). These saws are used for cutting curves such as the irregular edges of cut-outs. The smallest or **keyhole** blade and the medium or **compass** blade are the only ones used. The large blade, called a **pruning** blade, merely comes with the set.

Hacksaw (for 10″ blade, 45¢ each; blades, 10¢ each) used to saw metal. The blades are placed in the frame with the teeth pointing forward.

Circular Saw (8″ *Delta* make, No. 878, $40.35; ½ horse power motor No. 9000, $31.85). Advanced groups will find a power-driven circular saw very valuable. The above price includes accessories needed for scene building. The ⅓ horse power motor generally sold with this saw is not strong enough for heavy work. A circular saw is dangerous as well as useful, and precautions must be taken to keep irresponsible people from using it to cut their fingers off.

Miter Box (3″, $2.00 each) used as a guide when cutting molding at an angle. The homemade type shown at "D" p. 69 will answer all the needs of most groups.

Canvas Knife ** (small paring knife or a large jackknife, 10¢ to 50¢ each) employed for trimming canvas after it has been applied to a flat.

Drawknife (10″, $1.35 each) a blade with handles at each end, used for roughly trimming the edges of wood.

Plane (8″ long, 1⅝″ blade, $1.50 each) used for trimming the edges of lumber.

Chisels (¼″ and ½″ firmer type, 60¢ each) for digging rectangular holes in wood. Rarely used for amateur work.

Wood Rasp (14″, $1.40 each; handles, 5¢ each) used to roughen the edge of a board that is to represent an irregular object.

Files (6″ flat type, 20¢ each; 10″, 30¢ each; 4″ triangular type, 13¢ each; handles, 5¢ each). Flat files are used to smooth the rough edges left when metal has been cut. Triangular files are used to sharpen bits and other equipment.

Tin Snips (10″, 75¢ each) a type of heavy scissors for cutting tin.

Driving Tools

Accessories used in both driving and withdrawing nails and screws are included.

Hammer ** (ripping type 16 oz., 65¢ each). The ripping hammer has its claws at almost a right angle to the handle. It is better balanced than the old-fashioned claw hammer and is especially well adapted to pulling nails. Provide one hammer for each two workers.

Tack-hammer (magnetic type 4 oz., 95¢ each) generally preferred for driving tacks.

Stapling Machine † (sometimes called a **Tacker,** *Markwell* make, R B 5 Hard, $6.50 each) a special machine for driving staples. These staples may be substituted for tacks in temporary work where their lack of holding power is a real advantage. In spite of its cost a stapling machine is a valuable tool. The special staples needed with this machine (type R B) cost $2.75 per 5000.

Clenching Plates **. The nails used in flat construction are driven all the way through the wood and bent over, or **clenched,** on the far side. "F" p. 69 shows how this is done by putting an iron plate under the work and driving the nail against it. As far as I know, clenching plates are not manufactured and must be made up by some local iron worker. They should cost very little, but in some parts of the country it is hard to find iron of the right size and thickness. Theoretically the plates are right triangles ⅛″ thick and 12″ on a side, but any shape about this size will do. They should be thick enough to resist bending when the nails are driven against them, but not so thick that they throw the work out of line when they are placed under it. In many ways the blade of an old hacksaw makes as good a clenching plate as can be found. Two or three clenching plates are required for the average tool kit.

Wrecking Bar (2′ 0″ x ¾″, 30¢ each) a short iron bar with a crook at one end, used for pulling large nails. Never needed for light work.

Screwdriver ** (*Perfect Handle* type 4″ blade, 29¢ each) used for driving and removing screws, bolts, etc. In ordinary carpentry it is considered bad practice to use a screwdriver as a prying lever, but the scene builder employs his constantly for this and other unorthodox purposes. On this account a good quality screwdriver of the type listed is a necessity. Ordinary screwdrivers will not last a day. A screwdriver for each two workers will be required.

Spiral Ratchet Screwdriver † (spring return type 20″ long when extended, including bit, $3.50 each) works by being pushed against the head of the screw. Although this variety of screwdriver is not essential, the scene builder will find it the most useful tool he can buy. However it will not entirely take the place of ordinary screwdrivers, and one or two of the latter must be included in the tool kit.

Sure Shot Punch (*Trimble & Fink Mfg. Co.*, Baltimore, Md. 25¢ each) a handy little device for setting screws in the exact center of the holes in hardware.

Boring Tools

Boring tools are used for making round holes in wood or metal.

Brace ** (10″ ratchet type, $1.00 each) generally spoken of as a "brace and bit" although the bits are separate and interchangeable.

Bits ** (⁷⁄₁₆″, 45¢ each) used for boring holes for **lash-line** (p. 127) or for ⅜″ carriage bolts. Other sizes may be needed for special purposes.

Hand Drill (egg-beater type with ¼″ chuck, 75¢ each) used with straight-shank twist-drills for boring small holes. Much faster than a brace.

Power Hand Drill (*Thor* make, U-17-A, with ½″ capacity **Jacob's chuck,** $40.00). Advanced groups will find this drill a worthwhile purchase. Its small size combined with the large capacity chuck (which holds the twist-drills) makes it adaptable to every stage use.

Twist-drills ** (⁷⁄₃₂″ square-shank type for brace, 23¢ each; straight-shank type for hand or power drill, 17¢ each) used for boring holes to take No. 9 screws or ³⁄₁₆″ stove bolts. Other sizes may be needed for special purposes.

Countersink * (½″ for metal, 15¢ each) made either with

square shank for use with a brace, or with a straight shank for use with a hand or power drill. Used to **countersink** holes in metal so that screw heads will fit flush with the surface.

Automatic Drill † (type with magazine handle to hold drill points, $2.50 each) works by merely pushing point against wood. Used chiefly for boring holes to start screws. This drill takes special drill points which come in sets of eight and sell for 85¢ a set.

Center-punch (⅜" x 6", 30¢ each). A metal drill must be "started" by making a small indentation. This is done by placing the punch on the desired spot and striking it with a hammer.

Gripping Tools

The cheapest grade of gripping tools is sufficient for stage work since they are not often needed.

Vise * (type combining vise, pipe-vise, and anvil, 3" jaws, $2.30 each) rarely used but a necessity for sawing and bending metal. If the occasional use of a vise can be obtained there is no need to purchase one.

Machinist's Pliers * (6½", 10¢ each; 10", 60¢ each) used for tightening nuts, cutting wires, etc.

Pipe Wrenches * (14", 75¢ each) used for handling pipe and pipe fittings. Two such wrenches are needed, one to grasp the pipe and one to twist the fitting.

Miscellaneous Tools

These implements hardly deserve to be called tools, but they are listed here because they are all used in building scenery.

Paste Brush ** (oval varnish brush, 85¢ each) used in applying canvas to flats, etc.

Varnish Brush * (2½", 40¢ each) for varnishing **profile blocks** (p. 58).

Upholsterer's Needle * (curved type 6", 10¢ each) for sewing canvas to scene-units of irregular shape.

CHAPTER VI

MATERIALS

The items commonly used in stagecraft are listed here with some comment on their special characteristics. (See p. 104 for painters' supplies.) The specifications as to size, type, etc., are merely guides and the reader will have to decide whether or not they apply to any particular case. An approximate price for each article is quoted so that some idea of the cost of scenery can be formed. Actual prices will vary, depending on the locality, the quantity bought, special discounts, etc. When brand names are mentioned it means that I have had a long and satisfactory experience with the products in question and does not imply that other brands are inferior.

A knowledge of materials is as important as any other phase of stagecraft. Certainly the beginner's mistakes in selecting materials cause him more trouble than any other one factor.

Covering Materials

We think of scenery as something built, but actually the important part of scenery, like the important part of a picture, is the canvas, not the frame.

Draperies. In buying draperies or drapery materials, we should consider price, opacity, durability, and surface texture. Translucent materials must be lined to keep backstage lights from showing through them. Durability is of the utmost importance, as theater drapes have to stand more than their share of abuse. Cyclorama units are made of plain material as they must serve as backgrounds for all types of scenes.

The cheapest practical drapery material is **cotton flannel** which can be had in the **outing** grade for 15¢ a square yard retail. The better **Domet** grade costs 19¢. The best material at a reasonable price is **cotton velvet,** which can be bought *made up into draperies* for about $1.00 a square yard. No. 10 (½″) jack chain, which may be purchased at the hardware store for 3¢ per foot, is used to weight the bottoms of drapes.

Canvas. The most satisfactory fabric for covering flats, doors, and framed units in general is **canvas** (sometimes called **duck**). It should be bought in the 72″ width. In the 8 oz. weight, so named because each square yard weighs eight ounces, it is so sturdy that it will last for fifteen or twenty productions. Stock scenery should always be covered with canvas. Muslin, which is sometimes substituted, is far less economical. It tears easily and stagehands are always putting their shoulders through it. If canvas is purchased in 100-yard bolts, it may be had for only 2¢ or 3¢ a running yard more than the retail price of muslin.

John Boyle & Co., Inc., of 112 Duane St., New York, N.Y., make a canvas under the trade name of *Feltdux* that is ideal for scene building. The 72″ width is priced at from 24¢ to 37¢ a running yard depending on the cotton market. The bolts vary from 102 to 110 yards. The purchaser has to take whatever yardage (within these limits) fate deals out to him. Canvas is heavy and should be ordered two or three weeks in advance in order to take advantage of freight rates which may be as much as $10.00 a bolt cheaper than express. Less than bolt lots can be bought at 5¢ a running yard over the bolt price.

If flameproofed canvas is required, it may be bought from *The Astrup Company, Inc.,* 39 Walker St., New York, N.Y., for 10¢ or 12¢ a yard above the Boyle Co.'s price for *Feltdux.* The treated material comes in 50-yard bolts and is only 69″ wide due to shrinkage.

Wire, etc. Three-dimensional trees and rocks owe their irregular shapes to **poultry netting,** commonly called **chicken wire.** The size with a 2″ mesh is the best. It comes in 50′ 0″ rolls from 12″ to 72″ in width and costs from 65¢ to $2.65 per roll. **Poultry netting staples** (10¢ lb.) are used to fasten the netting to the wooden framework of the tree, etc.

Window glass is usually omitted entirely but may be simulated by **wire screen** if desired. This should be bought in the

No. 14 mesh. It comes in widths from 24″ to 48″ and costs 3¢ per square foot. When leaded panes are called for, they can be easily outlined with **twilled tape,** which comes in 7-yard rolls at 10¢ each and may be bought at any notion counter.

Gauze. Drops used for fog, soft focus effects, etc., are made of **gauze,** also called **bobbinet** or **scrim.** This is not the "theatrical gauze" sold for window curtains, but is an entirely different fabric with an hexagonal weave. Gauze comes in white, light buff, dark blue, and black. The lighter shades produce stronger effects than the darker ones. It comes 30′ 0″ wide and in any length. A running yard (3′ 0″ x 30′ 0″) costs $3.00. If gauze drops are torn, they can be darned with ordinary thread, but they are so fragile that they will rarely last for more than two or three productions.

Padding used on platform tops may be cotton batting which costs almost nothing. Jute rug padding is slightly better and costs 2½¢ a square foot. A higher grade of rug padding, known as the **waffle** type, costs 6¢ or more per square foot.

Wallboard and plywood are used for such purposes as the edges of cut-outs and for covering curved flats. Wallboard comes in 4′ 0″ widths and in lengths from 6′ 0″ to 12′ 0″. The cheapest type costs about 3½¢ a square foot and for stage purposes is as good as the most expensive. If the set does not have to be shifted **corrugated board** which comes in 3′ 0″ x 3′ 0″ sheets (15¢ each) may be used instead of wallboard for cut-outs. The corrugated board is not very sturdy, but it is cheap and may be cut to any shape with a knife. Heavy plywood is not suited to stage needs, but a light type made of white pine or basswood and called **profile board** is very satisfactory. Unfortunately it is also expensive, so amateurs can rarely afford it except for profile-blocks (p. 58). The 7/32″ or 1/4″ thickness is the most useful. Profile board differs from common plywood only in the type of wood employed in its construction.

Lumber

By far the greatest part of the scene budget goes for lumber. For this reason many amateur groups buy cheap woods. This is a serious mistake. Poor lumber is unsatisfactory from start to finish. Even a piece of scenery that is to be used only once may be economically built of good lumber since the wood can be salvaged when the scene is taken apart. Cheap lumber splits badly, so its salvage value is small. Good lumber costs three or four times as much as the cheapest wood you could use, but its greater durability will repay the difference many times over.

Lumber Sizes and Prices. The various sizes of lumber are named from their thickness and width *before they are planed*. For example, when we speak of a 1″ x 3″ (read "one by three") we mean a piece of lumber that was 1″ thick and 3″ wide in the rough. Planing, or **finishing** as it is usually called, decreases the size of the lumber so that the 1″ x 3″ that we buy is actually only about ¾″ x 2⅝″. Unfortunately, finished lumber sizes are not uniform. This does not matter in the larger sizes, but in the smaller ones it is important. A piece of wood that measures ⅞″ x 2¾″ will not work well with another that is ¾″ x 2⅝″. This point should be taken up with the dealer and the exact actual dimensions for each nominal size fixed. The nominal sizes most frequently called for are listed below under "Woods."

Lumber comes in lengths of from 8′ 0″ to 20′ 0″ in 2′ 0″ steps. Lengths under 10′ 0″ or over 16′ 0″ may cost more or be hard to find. For most stage purposes it makes little difference whether the lumber is 12′ 0″, 14′ 0″ or 16′ 0″ long.

Lumber prices are figured by the **board foot** which is 1″ x 12″ x 12″. Calculations are based on the nominal sizes. Thus there are two feet of 1″ x 6″, four feet of 1″ x 3″, or one and a half feet of 2″ x 4″ in a board foot. Some lumber yards do not price the smaller sizes in this way and in practice it is well to get a quotation per running foot for each of the standard sizes. This eliminates argument and simplifies cost calculations.

Woods. The heavier scene-units such as steps and platforms may be built of any wood that is available, cheap, reasonably strong and straight. My own experience has been limited to **yellow pine, fir,** and **spruce.** Spruce is particularly good but hard to find. The other two are about equal. Prices vary widely in different parts of the country but a No. 2 grade yellow pine, which is good enough for most stage purposes, should not cost over $3\frac{1}{2}$¢ a board foot. These woods are used in the following sizes:

Called 1″ x 6″, actually about $\frac{3}{4}$″ x $5\frac{5}{8}$″
" 1″ x 10″, " " $\frac{3}{4}$″ x $9\frac{5}{8}$″
" 1″ x 12″, " " $\frac{3}{4}$″ x $11\frac{5}{8}$″
" 2″ x 4″, " " $1\frac{5}{8}$″ x $3\frac{5}{8}$″

All other scenery, including flats, doors, windows, ceilings, etc., requires lumber that is light, straight, easy to work, and not inclined to split. The only common wood that meets these specifications is **white pine,** which is used in the following sizes:

Called 1″ x 2″, actually about $\frac{3}{4}$″ x $1\frac{5}{8}$″
" 1″ x 3″, " " $\frac{3}{4}$″ x $2\frac{5}{8}$″
" 1″ x 4″, " " $\frac{3}{4}$″ x $3\frac{5}{8}$″
" 1″ x 6″, " " $\frac{3}{4}$″ x $5\frac{5}{8}$″
" $1\frac{1}{4}$″ x 3″, " " 1″ x $2\frac{5}{8}$″

Of these sizes, only the 1″ x 2″, 1″ x 3″, and 1″ x 6″ are often needed. The 1″ x 4″ is used chiefly for the battens on large drops, and the $1\frac{1}{4}$″ x 3″ is employed to frame pieces that need special strength such as tormentors and large ceilings. All sizes are purchased in 12′ 0″, 14′ 0″ or 16′ 0″ lengths. **Random lengths** (which means that the lumber yard sends whatever lengths it has) are somewhat cheaper than specified lengths and work out just as well.

Unfortunately white pine is expensive. The best grade costs 12¢ a board foot. Even at this price it is strongly recommended. Scenery built from it is better in every way than that constructed from cheaper wood and is so durable that the extra expense is more than justified in the long run. However, it is rarely necessary to purchase the best grade.

Lumber grades are supposed to be standard throughout the United States but there are variations. Besides, each yard stocks only one or two grades and these differ with the locality. These factors make it impossible to recommend a particular grade. Nevertheless, the following information should enable your lumber dealer to furnish you with the cheapest grade he carries that will meet your needs:

The 1″ x 2″s and 1″ x 3″s are used for framing light structures that must be straight and able to withstand rough treatment. This does not mean that every piece of wood bought in these sizes needs to be straight and free from knots. A slight curve in a 16′ 0″ strip will not show after it is cut into pieces 4′ 0″ or 5′ 0″ long, nor will a bad knot 5′ 0″ from the end of a 14′ 0″ strip keep three 4′ 0″ pieces from being sawed out of it.

Summed up, this means that 1″ x 2″ and 1″ x 3″ should be ordered in a grade that contains a fair percentage of pieces that are straight for at least 12′ 0″ of their length (16′ 0″ pieces usually run this way) ; that includes no badly twisted pieces ; and that does not allow too many knots.

The 1″ x 6″s should be straight but may contain tight knots 1″ or less in diameter.

To meet these specifications, one dealer furnished me with a good grade of 1″ x 2″s and 1″ x 3″s, and a medium grade of 1″ x 6″s. My present dealer sells me what he calls **shop grade** which comes in random widths and lengths. He rips it into the widths I need and gives it to me for 8¢ a board foot. By a little care in cutting, I can make use of this lumber with only about 10% waste and still save more than 3¢ a board foot over the price of the next cheapest white pine available in my locality.

The only common wood that compares in quality with white pine is **cypress,** which sells for about the same price. I have had no personal experience with it. Opinions differ as to its value, though I have heard it recommended for damp climates. If your lumber yard suggests **ponderosa pine,** pay no attention. It is relatively heavy, hard to work, and easily split.

Profile-blocks (p. 73) are the secret of flat construction. They are used for joining the structural members. As their name indicates, they are cut from the light ¼″ plywood known as profile board. The two most common shapes are the **corner-block,** a right triangle 10″ on a side, and the **keystone** which is 8″ long and tapers from 4″ at one end to 3″ at the other. Profile-blocks are usually beveled on one side to minimize splinters but this is not essential.

Readymade corner-blocks cost 8¢ each. Keystones are 5¢ each. They may be bought from *J. R. Clancy, Inc.,* Syracuse, N.Y. The amateur will save money if he owns, or can borrow, a power saw and cut his own profile-blocks.

Whether profile-blocks are made or bought, they should be given two coats of waterproof varnish. The life of most scenery depends on the glue in the profile-block. If this glue is destroyed by dampness, the block falls apart and the scene-unit is ruined.

Molding is used for trim and gives finish to a set. It is generally made of white pine. The shape shown on p. 91 is adaptable to every requirement. A saving can be effected by standardizing on this type of molding, since every piece matches every other piece and there is almost no waste. Although this shape is stock as far as the theater is concerned, it is unfortunately not stocked by lumber yards and must be made to order. This necessitates a **set-up** cost, usually $2.50, so money can be saved by ordering a fair quantity at one time.

In spite of its price, which is a little over 1¢ a running foot, molding is very economical as it permits almost 100% salvage. Even pieces 4″ and 5″ long can be saved and used again.

Lattice Strip, which is $\frac{5}{16}$″ x $1\frac{3}{8}$″ and costs $1\frac{1}{4}$¢ a foot, finds a number of miscellaneous uses. The dealer pays the same price for white pine stripping as for yellow and should charge no more for it.

Adhesives

Adhesives are used chiefly to hold canvas in place on flats. **Casein glue** is recommended for all permanent work. It comes in powdered form and must be mixed according to directions on the box just before using. It will spoil if left over night. The glue costs 65¢ a pound but a little goes a long way.

In most theaters there is a good deal of temporary canvassing that is expected to last only for a single production. For this purpose ordinary **cold water paste** (paper hanger's paste) which costs 15¢ per pound is ideal. It holds well, but not so well that canvas applied with it cannot easily be removed. To mix paste : put water in a pail and stir the paste into it a pinch at a time, making sure that each pinch is entirely dissolved before the next is added. When the ripples left on the surface by the stirring paddle do not level out, the paste is thick enough for use. It is impossible to get a smooth mixture if the water is added to the paste.

Hardware

Only a small part of the scene budget goes for hardware. The more expensive items can be used many times and the others are cheap.

Nails. The most important nail used in scene building is the **clout nail,** which resembles an old-fashioned cut nail in appearance. Clout nails are not used in ordinary carpentry and your hardware dealer will probably have to order them. They have little holding power unless driven all the way through the work and clenched on the far side ("F" p. 69). For this reason they should be about ¼" longer than the total materials to be joined. With ¾" lumber and ¼" profile-blocks the 1¼" clout nail does nicely. With greater thicknesses the 1½" nail must be used. Clout nails cost about 10¢ a pound if bought in fair quantity. Ten or fifteen pounds are enough to build a set of scenery.

Beginners sometimes try to build flats with **roofing nails.** Don't!

Ordinary **common** and **finishing nails** are used for general purposes. Their sizes are listed as 4d, 6d, etc. For "4d" we read "four penny," as this was originally the price per hundred of this size. Today "4d" simply means "size four" and is a matter of length; a 4d nail, for example, is 1½" long. Finishing nails are most used in the 4d, 6d, and 8d sizes. Common nails should also be bought in these sizes with a few pounds of the 2d and 16d sizes added. All these types of nails run from 5¢ to 7¢ per pound.

Many amateurs make the mistake of using **wiggle nails** (sometimes called **corrugated fasteners**). Wiggle nails make a quick, easy joint but are a curse from then on. They weaken the wood; they work out when you rely on them, but cannot be extracted intentionally by any known method; worst of all, they practically ruin lumber for salvage.

Tacks are needed to hold canvas in place. **Cut tacks** in the 8 oz. size (15¢ lb.) are the only kind for the purpose. **Wire tacks** are undesirable in every way.

Screws used on stage are nearly all of the **flat-head bright** type. The most common sizes are ⅞″ x 9 (read "seven-eighths by nine") and 1½″ x 9, although a few ¾″ x 5 screws are occasionally needed. The numbers "9" and "5" are sizes and refer to the diameter of the shank. No. 9 screws are ³⁄₁₆″ in diameter and No. 5 screws are ⅛″. The screws listed sell for from 20¢ to 40¢ a gross. Although they cost about seven times as much as nails, screws can be used over and over so the cost per use is low.

Bolts. Where extra strength is needed ³⁄₁₆″ **flat-head stove bolts** may be substituted for screws. The 2″ size (50¢ per 100) is the most useful, but the 2½″ (60¢ per 100) and the 3″ (75¢ per 100) sizes are occasionally needed. **Washers** for these bolts cost about 5¢ a hundred.

For heavy work, such as platform building, ⅜″ **carriage bolts** are employed. The 4″ length (2¢ each) and the 6″ length (3¢ each) are the sizes most frequently required. Washers to fit ⅜″ bolts cost 50¢ per hundred.

Hinges. Four types of hinges will answer most stage needs. Two of these types are twins: the **tight-pin** and the **loose-pin backflaps.** Both have square leaves and are alike except that the loose-pin type can be taken apart by removing its pin. The tight-pin variety may be bought at any hardware store for 20¢ a pair. The loose-pin kind (usually called a **pin-hinge**) is sold only as stage hardware and must be bought from *J. R. Clancy, Inc.* Both kinds should be purchased in the size that is 4⅜″ x 2″ when open.

The **strap hinge** (6″, heavy, 30¢ a pair) ranks next in importance. This is a diamond-shaped hinge of the type seen at "C" p. 87.

For hinging doors that swing onstage the 2½″ **tight-pin light steel butt hinge** is used. This is like the tight-pin backflap except that its leaves are rectangular. A pair costs 10¢.

Miscellaneous Regular Hardware. Any good hardware store can supply all the following materials, with the possible exception of the piano wire which may have to be purchased from a piano tuner. Only the first three items listed are needed in any quantity, but all are important and should be kept on hand if your group does any great amount of scene building.

NAME	SIZE, TYPE, ETC.	PRICE	REMARKS
Mending-plates	¾″ x 3″	20¢ doz.	Making joints, as a quick substitute for profile-blocks, or when lack of space or other conditions make these unsatisfactory.
Corner-plates	¾″ x 3½″	26¢ doz.	
Corner-irons	¾″ x 3″	50¢ doz.	
Screw eyes	No. 108 = ⅜″	10¢ doz.	Used for attaching ropes, cords, etc. to light scenery. Nos. 105 & 108 are stronger than Nos. 5 & 10. Dimensions refer to diameters of the eyes.
	No. 105 = ½″	15¢ doz.	
	No. 10 = ⅜″	5¢ doz.	
	No. 5 = ⅝″	8¢ doz.	
Wire hooks	2½″	15¢ doz.	The type used on screen doors. Used for holding light scenery together when a quick release is necessary.
Harness snaps	Medium	10¢ ea.	These are tied to the ends of ropes which must be attached or detached quickly.
Turnbuckles	½″ size 6″ opening	33¢ ea.	For tightening wire ("A" p. 21).
Turnbuttons	2″	1¢ ea.	For holding plugs in place ("B" p. 81).

Miscellaneous Regular Hardware (*Continued*)

Name	Size, Type, etc.	Price	Remarks
Wing-nuts	$\frac{3}{8}''$	2¢ ea.	Sometimes called thumb-nuts. Used instead of square nuts on platforms and other units that must be assembled and dismantled frequently.
Horizontal rim-locks	$3\frac{1}{8}'' \times 4$	40¢ ea.	The lock used on stage doors ("F" p. 87).
Strap iron	$\frac{3}{16}'' \times \frac{3}{4}''$	48¢ bar	Used for sill irons ("C" p. 81), comes in 20′ 0″ bars.
Stovepipe wire	12 gauge 50′ 0″ to a coil	10¢ coil	For tying netting together (p. 97).
Piano wire	26 gauge 96′ 0″ to a coil	$1.30 coil	The strongest wire made. Tensile strength 900 lbs.

Special Stage Hardware. Many of the supplies used on stage cannot be procured from hardware stores but must be ordered from *J. R. Clancy, Inc.,* of Syracuse, N.Y. This firm specializes in theatrical hardware, and good scenery can hardly be built without using some of its products. The methods of using these items will be dealt with at length in the later chapters, but I have grouped the items themselves on the following page for the convenience of the reader. The code numbers from Clancy's catalog are added for ready reference. This catalog (which the firm sends free on request) contains much valuable information and should be in the hands of every amateur scene builder.

Special Stage Hardware

Name	See Page	Catalog #	Cost	Purpose
Stage-screws	145	230	$5.80 doz.	Screwing scenery to the floor.
Footiron (solid)	145	42	.25 ea.	Attaching scenery to the floor.
Footiron (hinged)	131	142	.25 ea.	
Footiron (flat)	99	542	.12 ea.	
Brace-clamps	127	233	.70 set	Hardware for making stage-braces.
Brace-hook and rocker-heel	127	432	.60 set	
Brace-cleat (Scheel's)	127	438	.06 ea.	Attaching stage-braces to flats.
Lash-cleat (Wise's)	127	439	.06 ea.	Joining flats.
Lash-hooks (Towel's)	127	939	.05 ea.	Tying off lash-lines.
Floor plates (oblong)	141	298	.20 ea.	Rigging book ceilings.
Ceiling-plates (with rings)	141	98	.40 ea.	Joining and rigging roll ceilings.
Hanger-iron (top)	130	99	.25 ea.	Rigging flats to fly.
Hanger-iron (bottom)	130	199	.30 ea.	
Picture frame-hangers				
Large socket	130	577	.06 ea.	Hanging pictures and other light objects.
Large hook	130	677	.06 ea.	
Small socket	130	977	.04 ea.	
Small hook	130	1077	.04 ea.	
S-hooks	130	64	.06 ea.	Bracing flats.
Backflaps (loose-pin)	87	37	2.35 doz.	Hinging doors.
Mending-battens	98	450	.22 ea.	Large mending-plates for mending broken scenery.
Cyclorama knuckles (Tull's)	134	487-C	11.00 set	For joining cyclorama arms to pipe-batten.

Rigging Supplies

The equipment listed here is used primarily to shift scenery. However, most of it will prove valuable, and perhaps necessary, for a score of other purposes, chief of which is the hanging of ceilings and borders.

Pulleys for rigging may be the ordinary wood or metal blocks sold in hardware stores. They can be attached to the beams with rope, or better with chains. Single-sheave blocks cost from 65¢ to $1.80 each, and triple-sheave blocks from $1.55 to $4.00, depending on the size rope with which they are to be used. Special **loft-blocks** (p. 139), sold by *J. R. Clancy, Inc.,* bolt or clamp directly to the beams. These are better than the common blocks but cost from $1.30 to $5.00 apiece. For light rigging **swivel-eye cast-iron awning pulleys** with $1\frac{1}{4}''$ sheaves are good enough. They cost 12¢ each.

Rope. Two kinds of rope are employed on stage: twisted **manila,** and braided cotton (commonly called **sash cord**). Only the manila should be used to bear weight, as cotton is unreliable. Even manila loses its strength rapidly and should be replaced at least every two years if it is to be used where a break would cause damage.

Diame- ter	MANILA		SASH CORD	
	Safe Load (when new)	Cost per 100' 0''	Breaking Strength	Cost per 100' 0''
$\frac{1}{4}''$	120 lbs.	$0.59	450 lbs.	$0.65
$\frac{3}{8}''$	230 "	1.20		
$\frac{1}{2}''$	530 "	2.06	1000 "	5.58
$\frac{5}{8}''$	880 "	3.33		
$\frac{3}{4}''$	1080 "	4.06		
$1''$	1800 "	6.52		

Friction Tape ($\frac{3}{4}''$, comes in rolls of various sizes and costs about 1¢ a yard) is used to bind the ends of manila rope to keep them from unraveling.

Pipe, used for making pipe-battens, should be of steel and in the $1\frac{1}{4}''$ size. It comes in 20' 0" lengths which cost $3.00 each. Most battens are about 35' 0" long, so two lengths must be joined to make a batten. The joint is made with a **pipe coupling** into which the ends of the pipe screw. Couplings cost 11¢ each. **Caps,** which cost 16¢ each, should be screwed onto the ends of the battens. To keep the lines from slipping on the pipe, 1" **pipe straps** (p. 139, 1¢ each) are attached to the battens by means of stove bolts.

Sandbags may be bought from *J. R. Clancy, Inc.* They range in capacity from 10 lbs. to 200 lbs. and cost from 90¢ to $7.80 each. The bags are attached to the lines with Clancy's *Easy Trim* **clamps** (Catalogue No. 46). These cost $3.00 each.

Casters ("D" p. 145) are needed for scenery which is to be shifted by rolling. There are two types of casters, the **rigid** and the **swivel.** The rigid type can roll in either direction along one line but does not permit curves. Where this kind of movement is needed, rigid casters are much better than the swivel variety which, while they may be rolled in any direction, are likely to jam if used with a back-and-forth movement. Both types must be large, rubber-tired, and of good quality, since they will be subjected to strains under which small or poor casters will fail to function.

The *Faultless* caster made by *Noelting Company* of Evansville, Indiana, is quite satisfactory for most purposes in the "regular duty" grade. The best size has a $3\frac{1}{8}''$ wheel. The swivel type (catalog No. 121–3) costs $1.40 each. The rigid type (catalog No. 521–3) costs $1.10 each.

CHAPTER VII

BUILDING METHODS

In this chapter all the important scene-units are described and their structure illustrated. These units, with minor variations, make up at least 95% of all scenery. The methods used in their construction have an even wider application, so much so that—with the exception of a few forms which lie altogether outside the range of the amateur—almost any imaginable scenic element may be built by following the basic principles given here.

All the processes described are short cuts, whether or not they seem so at first glance. Any attempt at further simplification is likely to result in flimsy construction.

Carpentry. Stagecraft requires very little knowledge of woodworking, but the novice should understand the few points gathered here before going on to the more detailed instructions for building scene-units.

When measuring a board for cutting, check the end to see if it is square and free from cracks ("A" p. 69). If not, draw a line across it (using a try-square and a pencil) far enough back to allow a square cut, and to clear any imperfections in the wood. Sawing along this line gives a squared, sound end from which to begin measuring. As each measurement is made, the line of the cut should be marked with try-square and pencil. Any attempt to saw by eye will result in a botched job. If two or more pieces are to be cut from the same board, it is necessary to mark a space between them for the saw cut. A handsaw makes a cut about $\frac{1}{16}''$ wide.

Structural members in amateur work are almost always **butt joined.** This means that the free ends are merely brought together at right angles or end-to-end ("B") without any fancy woodworking whatever. Of course, such a "joint" has no strength and must be held together by fastening a piece of wood or metal over the crack. Pieces that have been beveled or are otherwise irregular in cross-section cannot be joined in this way and must be **mitered** ("C"). This is done by cutting one end of each piece at half the angle at which they come together. In most cases the parts are perpendicular and the miter is therefore cut at 45°. The miter joint is used principally in working with molding.

In planning the structure of a scene-unit, remember that nails and screws driven into the end-grain of a piece of wood have almost no holding power. Often this makes a great deal of difference in the design of the unit. The framework of the stairs ("D" p. 95) furnishes a good example of this. For very light work an exception to this rule may be made (e. g. the molding at "E" p. 91).

If a piece of metal is to be held in place by screws, the screw holes are **reamed out** to a conical shape which permits the screw heads to fit flush with the surface. This process is called **countersinking.** When screws are used in soft wood their heads will countersink themselves. When things other than screw heads are said to be countersunk, it means that the material below them is cut away so that they can be placed flush with the surface.

When drilling metal the drill must be constantly lubricated with automobile oil; otherwise its temper will be lost.

Dismantling Scenery. Although the process of taking scenery apart may seem to have little to do with building it, there is a fundamental connection. Except for such stock items as flats, doors, etc. most scene-units are dismantled after the last performance of a production in order that the materials they contain may be salvaged. This requires a type of construction that depends on screws and bolts to hold its joints together. Nails, as a rule, either hold too well or let go too easily. I worked with one carpenter who had the habit of joining his scenery with nails driven from every possible angle with the result that it took as long to dismantle a unit as it did to build it, and half the wood was split in the process.

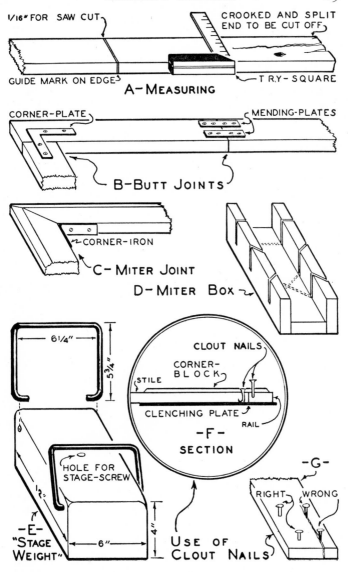

1/16" FOR SAW CUT

GUIDE MARK ON EDGE

CROOKED AND SPLIT
END TO BE CUT OFF

TRY-SQUARE

A—MEASURING

CORNER-PLATE

MENDING-PLATES

B—BUTT JOINTS

CORNER-IRON

C—MITER JOINT

D—MITER BOX

6 1/4"

5 3/4"

HOLE FOR
STAGE-SCREW

—E—
"STAGE
WEIGHT"

6"

4"

CLOUT NAILS

CORNER-
BLOCK

STILE

CLENCHING PLATE

RAIL

—F—
SECTION

USE OF
CLOUT NAILS

—G—

RIGHT   WRONG

Hung Scenery

Hung scenery depends for its shape on gravity and hence is the simplest of all types.

Drapes of expensive materials are best made by an expert, but cheap ones present no difficulty to anyone who can operate a sewing machine. The seams should run vertically. No side hems are necessary as the selvage prevents fraying. The top hem should be 2″ deep and reinforced with 2″ webbing on the back. In this hem are placed ⅜″ metal eyelets called **grommets.** This requires a special tool, and, while the amateur can do the work himself, it will probably be cheaper to have the grommets installed by an awning maker. The first grommet should be placed in an upper corner of the material, the next 12″ away, the next 6″, then 12″, then 6″, and so on. This makes it possible to hang the drapes in a modified **French pleat** if desired. The bottom hems of all drapes should be weighted with No. 10 (½″) jack chain.

Borders of the type used with a cyclorama set in place of a ceiling are usually made of some soft material to match the cyclorama itself and are hung in folds. Canvas borders such as the foliage borders shown on pp. 33 and 99 are hung flat. Note how the leaves are cut so that each is supported by the canvas immediately above it. Since the leaves may curl slightly, the bottom edge of the border should be painted on both sides to keep any bare canvas from showing. Borders in the commercial theater are often elaborately cut out and even supplied with holes. This is supposed to increase the realism of the effect. Unfortunately, such a border must be reinforced by heavy netting which is quite visible to the audience and more than destroys the advantage gained. The amateur will do well to make his foliage borders like the one shown, and keep them inconspicuous by hanging them as high as possible and not lighting them too brightly. There is no such thing as a convincing border, and attempts to improve them only call attention to their defects.

Borders are usually provided with battens ("B" p. 99). This type of batten is in two halves with the top edge of the canvas sandwiched between them. Each half is made of two (sometimes more) lengths of 1″ x 3″, or, in the case of the very large borders, 1″ x 4″. The canvas is first glued and tacked to the back half and then the front half is put on and bolted in place. A joint in front should never come opposite a joint in back or the batten will be fatally weak at this point. It is well to strengthen joints by bolting a large mending-plate over them.

When not in use, the border is rolled up on the batten. The ends of all bolts must be cut off with a hacksaw and the nuts countersunk ("C") to keep them from tearing the canvas. It is also well to round off the edges of the batten.

Drops (p. 121) are made of two or more lengths of canvas sewed together with the seams running horizontally. An awning maker will do this work for about 10¢ a yard. After it is sewed, the drop should be laid on the stage floor and cut so that it tapers slightly from top to bottom. This taper, which amounts to about 1″ in 1′ 0″, helps to avoid the corner wrinkles that are common in rectangular drops.*

Drops have battens at both top and bottom. These are made and attached like those described for borders.

Flat Construction

Given a knowledge of the materials to use, anyone can learn to make a good flat from a study of the drawings on pp. 73, 77, and 81. Nevertheless, their inherent simplicity does not diminish the importance of the methods used. There are a number of short cuts that are well worth knowing, and also certain difficulties to be avoided. Furthermore, the processes employed in flat building are fundamental. Once they are mastered, the construction of the remaining scene-units will follow naturally.

Cutting. Since the structure of a flat does not depend on its width and is influenced only in minor details by its height, we can simplify our description by taking a specific example. Let us choose a flat 12′ 0″ high and 5′ 9″ wide. The lumber

* *Scenery for the Theatre*, Burris-Meyer & Cole.

used will be 1″ x 2″ and 1″ x 3″ white pine. We begin by checking our wood, making sure that it is reasonably straight and that it is all the same actual size. Let us suppose that we have done this and found the 1″ x 2″ to be actually ¾″ x 1⅝″ and the 1″ x 3″ to be ¾″ x 2⅝″. This checking is essential, since our calculations will depend on the exact dimensions of the lumber we use.

The top and bottom members are known as **rails.** As the sketch shows, these run the full width of the flat. This is important, since it gives the flat a smooth surface to slide on when it is moved. Our first step, therefore, is to cut two pieces of 1″ x 3″ that are 5′ 9″ long, taking care to get the dimensions exact and the ends square.

The uprights, called **stiles,** are also of 1″ x 3″. They are shorter than the height of the flat by the combined height of the rails; hence we make them 11′ 6¾″ (12′ 0″ − 2 × 2⅝″). The central member, or **toggle-bar,** also of 1″ x 3″, is shorter than the rails by the width of the stiles. Subtracting 2 × 2⅝″ from 5′ 9″ gives us 5′ 3¾″ for the length of the toggle-bar. In cases like these where one piece of lumber runs past or overlaps another, it is said to **carry through.** Thus the rails carry through where they join the stiles, and the stiles carry through where they join the toggle-bar.

The **corner-braces** are made of 1″ x 2″. Their ends are cut at an angle of 45° so that they will fit against the stile and rail. This not only makes a neat job but is essential for strength as well. Corner-braces are not cut, as a rule, until after the main members of the flat are joined. They are usually about as long as the rails, but must be made shorter in proportion for narrow flats. Their lengths need not be exact and can be judged by eye. Beginners frequently make the mistake of placing the braces in diagonally opposite corners. The proper arrangement is shown in the drawing.

Flats over 12′ 0″ high require two toggle-bars. Flats over 14′ 0″ should be built of 1¼″ x 3″ (white pine).

Squaring. A flat must have square corners; otherwise it is worthless. It will not fit with other flats and will cause trouble as long as it lasts. Squaring is not hard, but it does take

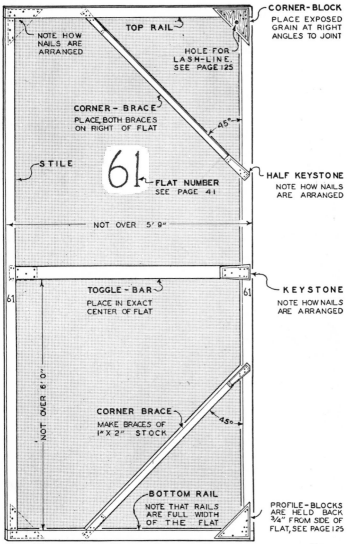

BACK VIEW OF PLAIN FLAT — SHOWING CONSTRUCTION OF FRAME

pains. The directions given here may seem unnecessarily detailed, but if followed carefully, they will eliminate many difficulties.

Starting with a stile, we lay it flat on the floor and nail one end down with two 4d common nails. One nail should be about 1' 0" from the end of the stile, and the second 1' 6" or 2' 0" from the first. These nails are only temporary and should not be driven home. Now we go to the far end of the stile and sight along it to see if it is straight. If it is not, we straighten it, and hold it in place with another nail. These temporary nails should not be set where they will later interfere with the profile-blocks.

One rail is then put in place and squared with a steel square. Make sure that the end of the rail is flush with the outside of the stile. Nail the rail to the floor and proceed in the same way with the remaining stile and rail, making sure that the members are straight and that the corners are exactly flush and square.

No matter how carefully this work has been done, the fourth corner will sometimes fail to square. When this happens the whole frame must be checked. Perhaps a stile is not straight; perhaps a corner slipped before it was nailed; perhaps one of the members is not quite the right length. Even a small error will cause trouble when working with an object as large as a flat, but that is nothing to the trouble it will cause if it is not discovered until after the flat is built. As a final test, it is well to measure the diagonals with a piece of string. If they are the same, we may be reasonably sure that our flat is square.

Joining the members of a flat frame is accomplished by nailing profile-blocks over the joints with clout nails.

Corner-blocks are used for attaching the rails to the stiles. They should be about ¼" from the outer edge of the rail and exactly ¾" from the outer edge of the stile. The exposed grain of the block must run at right angles to the joint. To understand the reason for this, try bending a corner-block in your hands. It bends easily along the grain, but is very strong and rigid across the grain. Keystones are used to hold the toggle-bar in place while half-keystones will do for corner-braces.

Profile-blocks are placed about ¼″ from the outside edge of the rails and exactly ¾″ from the outside edge of the stiles. This last is called **holding back** the blocks. Note how one corner must be cut off the half-keystones to make it possible. The reason for holding back will be explained on p. 125.

Clout nails are the *only* type that should be used in flat construction. Note that the point of each nail is not round but is flat like a wedge. It is less likely to split the lumber if the line of the wedge is placed across the grain ("G" p. 69 *). A clenching plate is placed under the joint and the nails are driven through the block, through the wood, and clenched against the plate ("F" p. 69). If properly clenched, it is almost impossible to get them out. For this reason, when temporary units are joined with profile-blocks, ⅞″ x 9 screws must be substituted for nails.

The pattern in which the nails are driven is extremely important. Nails driven at random have little holding power, but a properly placed nail exercises a sort of jiujitsu; it applies its strength just where it is needed. One nail is placed in each corner of the block. Then two are driven on each side of the crack of the joint. Other nails are placed where needed. The complete patterns for the standard blocks are shown on p. 73.

Canvassing. The canvas of a flat covers only the front of the frame and is not carried around the edge and attached to the back in the manner favored by artists and sign painters.

To canvas a flat we first lay the frame face up on the floor. The canvas—which should be about three inches longer and an inch or more wider than the flat—is then placed on the frame with the selvage running along the outer edge of one stile. A temporary tack is now driven in each corner to hold the canvas in place. At this stage the material ought to be slack but not wrinkled and the threads should lie parallel with the stiles and rails. We now proceed to fasten the canvas to the first stile with a row of tacks driven 6″ apart and ¼″ from the inside edge of the stile. The canvas should not be drawn tight

* After *Scenery for the Theatre,* Burris-Meyer & Cole.

between the tacks as it will shrink later when painted. It is well for the novice to drive his tacks only half way in at first. This will make it easier to correct any mistakes that may creep in.

A row of tacks is now set along the other stile in the same manner, special care being taken to avoid diagonal wrinkles. The canvas should not be stretched but should hang slack to provide for shrinkage. Unfortunately, the exact amount of slackness cannot be specified as the shrinkage factor of canvas varies from bolt to bolt. This is not as serious as it sounds and practice will soon enable the builder to handle his canvas by "feel." We next tack the canvas to the rails, but here, in order to assure smoothness, we follow a slightly different procedure. The first tack is driven into the center of the rail ¼″ from the inside edge. We then place tacks in the centers of the spaces on either side, then in the centers of these spaces. (See "A" p. 77, where the numbers show the order in which the tacks are driven.) This process, which divides the canvas evenly, is repeated along the other rail.

We now have a rectangle of canvas attached to the frame by a row of tacks running around the inside edge of the stiles and rails. Outside this row is a flap of canvas which must now be glued to the wood. Casein glue is used and a liberal coat is applied to the back of the flap and the faces of the stiles and rails. We then smooth the flap into place with a small block of wood and set the flat away to dry.

When the glue has set, we examine our canvas to make sure there are no serious wrinkles. If there are any, we may have to pull part of the canvas free and correct them, but if not we can drive our first row of tacks home and run a second row, 1′ 0″ apart this time, around the outside of the flat face and about ½″ from the edge. (This row is shown on the right side of "A" near the hands.)

The waste canvas is now trimmed off and our flat is finished. The trimming is done with a knife as shown in the sketch. The knife does not really cut the canvas but acts rather as a ripping aid. Do not saw with it. The real trick lies in pulling the waste canvas away with the left hand at just

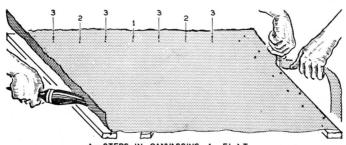

A — STEPS IN CANVASSING A FLAT

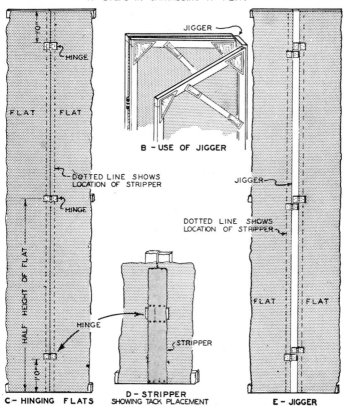

C — HINGING FLATS

B — USE OF JIGGER

D — STRIPPER
SHOWING TACK PLACEMENT

E — JIGGER

the right tension and at just the right angle. Once learned it is very quick.

Canvas should not be glued and tacked to the toggle-bars or to the corner-braces.

Hinging. Since a wall wider than 5′ 9″ is made up of two or more flats, it is necessary to hinge these flats together. "C" p. 77 shows how this is done. The hinges are tight-pin backflaps held in place with ⅞″ x 9 screws. Three hinges are used between each two flats. One is placed a foot from the top, one in the middle, and one a foot from the bottom. The pins of the hinges must be exactly over the crack and in line with it.

If three flats the same size are hinged together and one of the outside flats is folded, its free edge extends all the way to the crack between the other two flats. This makes it impossible to close the other outside flat. To avoid this difficulty, a piece of 1″ x 3″ the same height as the flat is used. This is called a **jigger** ("B" and "E"). It is hinged between two of the flats just as if it were a flat itself. The jigger gives a little play in the joint and permits the three flats to be folded. Four flats can be hinged together, if a jigger is placed in the middle. Even five flats can be hinged in this way, although in this case the location of the jigger must be worked out on paper, since it depends on the size of the flats. In difficult cases two jiggers may be necessary.

Strippers. When two flats are hinged together, the unsightly crack between them must be covered with a strip of canvas called a **stripper.** This should be a little longer than the crack and about 4″ wide (7″ when used over a jigger). It is first wet and then wrung out until it is only damp. Then it is laid on a piece of 1″ x 6″ and smeared with paste. (The 1″ x 6″ is used to keep the floor clean.) Paste is also brushed along the crack of the flat. The stripper is now turned over and applied to the crack. This usually takes two workers, one at each end. The stripper must not be stretched. One end is placed flush with the bottom of the flat. The overhang at the other end is turned under and pasted down. The paste brush, wiped fairly dry, can be used to smooth the stripper in place.

The paste must be reinforced with tacks. Four of these are placed at the top, four at the bottom, and four around each hinge ("D"). Note that the stripper does not completely cover the hinges. A stripper that is too wide is certain to come loose.

Most strippers are expected to hold for only one production. When permanence is desired, as in a convertible set, casein glue should be used instead of paste. Furthermore, the stripper should be held in place with four rows of tacks, two on each stile. This is important, as a stripper that comes loose after it has been painted cannot be re-attached without staining the paint.

Curved walls are built on a framework of the type shown at "B" p. 83. Four uprights are used which should be of white pine. The curved pieces, or **sweeps,** are generally made of yellow pine, because small pieces of this sort are useless as salvage. Note that they are made of several pieces bolted together. If single boards were used, they would often have to be two or more feet wide. Wallboard is employed for the covering material, which means that the curve cannot be more than 4' 0" wide. If the wallboard is covered on both sides with canvas, it can be bent in sharp curves without breaking. For gentle curves this is not necessary. Wallboard may be merely attached to the center uprights with 2d finishing nails, but should be screwed to the side uprights as it may pull loose if not securely fastened.

Door and Window Flats

Flats with openings such as those used to take door or window frames, fireplaces, etc., are more elaborate than plain flats. The framework for such flats is shown on p. 81. Notice how the main toggle-bar is raised and how two **inner stiles,** one on each side of the opening, are provided. Note also the small toggle-bars. These last are very important, as the inner stiles need this additional bracing for rigidity.

On flats of this kind it is often necessary to cut off parts of profile-blocks, so that they will fit in the space available.

Sill Irons. The principal feature of a door flat is the **sill**

iron. This is a piece of $\frac{3}{16}'' \times \frac{3}{4}''$ strap iron with 9'' on each end turned up. The iron can be bent cold by merely putting it in a vise and hitting it with a hammer. The outer dimension of the iron after bending must be exactly the width of the flat.

Since the iron is $\frac{3}{16}''$ thick, the stiles on a door flat must be $\frac{3}{16}''$ shorter than those on a plain flat. Note also that the lower ends of the stiles are countersunk to receive the bent parts of the iron. For the same reason the bottom rails are $\frac{3}{16}''$ shorter than they would otherwise be, and are rounded on the outside corners.

The iron is held in place by twelve $1\frac{1}{2}'' \times 9$ screws. Note the location of the screw holes in "C" and note also that screws are not placed in the end-grain of the rail. Use a $\frac{7}{32}''$ drill to bore the holes and then countersink them so that the heads of the screws will fit flush with the surface of the iron. When a flat is dragged along the floor, even a slight projection is a serious handicap.

Canvassing. Professionals cover door flats with a single piece of canvas, but a saving can be effected by using three pieces, one on each side of the opening and one at the top. If this method is followed, the top piece must be put on last so that it will overlap the lower pieces; otherwise the painters (who tend to work downward) will loosen the canvas with their brushes.

Plugs. Although it is possible to make special flats for windows, fireplaces, etc., it is more economical to make only door flats and then plug any part of the opening that is not needed.

One method of plugging ("D") is to cut two pieces of $1'' \times 3''$ the width of the opening and fasten them in place with mending-plates and corner-plates. (Note how the profile-blocks are held back $\frac{3}{4}''$ from the inside edge of the inner stiles to permit this.) These pieces and the inner stiles make a frame that can be covered with scrap canvas held in place with paste and tacks. The opening can be made still smaller by plugging it at the top and sides if desired. This requires more work but the principle is the same. "A" p. 43 shows a flat plugged for a fireplace.

A removable plug is illustrated at "B" p. 81. This par-

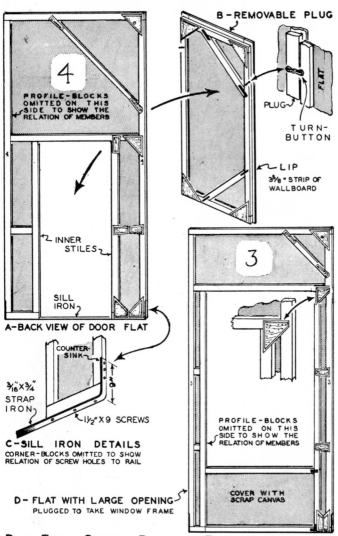

B — REMOVABLE PLUG

FLAT

PLUG

TURN-BUTTON

LIP
3⅜" STRIP OF WALLBOARD

4

PROFILE-BLOCKS OMITTED ON THIS SIDE TO SHOW THE RELATION OF MEMBERS

INNER STILES

SILL IRON

A — BACK VIEW OF DOOR FLAT

COUNTERSINK

3/16" × 3/4" STRAP IRON

9"

1½" × 9 SCREWS

C — SILL IRON DETAILS
CORNER-BLOCKS OMITTED TO SHOW RELATION OF SCREW HOLES TO RAIL

D — FLAT WITH LARGE OPENING
PLUGGED TO TAKE WINDOW FRAME

3

PROFILE-BLOCKS OMITTED ON THIS SIDE TO SHOW THE RELATION OF MEMBERS

COVER WITH SCRAP CANVAS

DOOR FLATS, SHOWING PLUGS AND PLUGGING METHODS.

ticular example is for turning a door flat of a convertible set into a plain flat, but the plugs that are part of the window and the fireplace on p. 10 are made on the same plan. Built like a small flat with its corner-braces joined with mending-plates, the plug has a **lip** of wallboard, 3⅝" wide, attached to its stiles and top rail with 2d common nails. This lip extends 1" past the edge of the plug so that it will cover the crack between the plug and the flat itself. The plug is not canvassed until after the lip is in place.

Arches are shown on p. 83. The Roman type, "A," is the simplest. The top part of the opening in the flat is covered with wallboard and a semicircle cut out of it ("C"). The straight thickness-pieces are made like small flats from 1" x 2". The curved thickness is a strip of wallboard, covered on both sides with canvas. If the arches are small, the thickness will fall naturally into the curve of the arch and the little **strut** in the center of the toggle-bar is all the support it needs. Large arches call for additional struts which will have to be carried on diagonals let into the opening above the curve.

The method used to make Gothic, Tudor and other special arches is shown at "D." The sweeps are first cut to the desired curve of the arch and fastened in place with mending-plates. **Spacer-blocks** ("E") are then made and screwed to the sweeps and to the inner stile of the flat. Next lattice strips are attached to the inside edges of the spacer-blocks. The lattice strips must first be scored with a number of parallel saw cuts to facilitate bending. The triangular spaces above the sweeps should be canvassed, but muslin is better for covering the thickness. Working around the curves requires care but it is not difficult.

Cut-outs

Flat scenery with irregular edges may be simple or complicated, depending on its design. The simple types use a flat as a basis ("D" p. 99) and attach a cut out edge of wallboard with 2d common nails. The wallboard should be cut

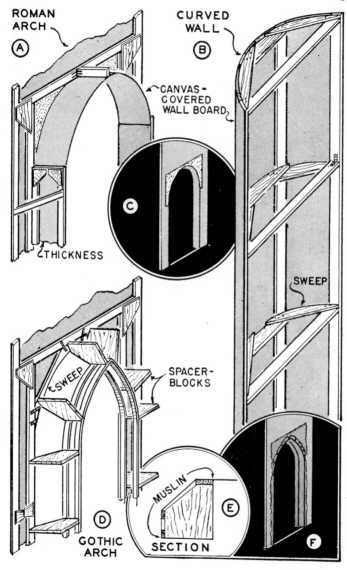

ROMAN ARCH Ⓐ

CURVED WALL Ⓑ

CANVAS-COVERED WALL BOARD

Ⓒ

THICKNESS

SWEEP

SPACER-BLOCKS

SWEEP

SWEEP

MUSLIN

Ⓔ

SECTION

Ⓓ GOTHIC ARCH

Ⓕ

before it is put in place. This can be done with a keyhole saw or a jig saw.

A 6″ or 8″ width of wallboard is about as much as can safely be trusted to stand alone. For projections greater than this, some sort of reinforcement should be added. The kind shown is particularly satisfactory. A piece of 1″ x 2″ is placed flat on the back of the wallboard, and a longer piece set up edgewise so that it runs from the outer end of the first piece of 1″ x 2″ to the far side of the flat. The whole arrangement is held in place by 1½″ x 9 screws driven in from the face.

A more elaborate cut-out is shown at "E" on the same page. The principal points to remember with this type are that the framing members (usually 1″ x 3″) should form triangles and that the main members must carry through. These requirements may necessitate slight alterations in the original design. Sometimes a change of even a few inches in an outline will permit great simplification of the framework. The wallboard should not project more than 8″ from the nearest support, and in any event should be kept down to a minimum. Wallboard is heavy and very difficult to keep in place if applied in large sheets. The whole face of the cut-out, wallboard and all, should be covered with canvas which can then be trimmed around the edges with a sharp knife.

Ceilings

There are two types of ceilings: the **roll ceiling,** so called because it may easily be taken apart and rolled up for storage, and the **book ceiling** which is like two huge flats hinged together.

Although both types may be framed with 1″ x 3″ white pine, 1¼″ x 3″ is definitely better in spite of its extra weight, as the former is a little flimsy.

Roll ceilings ("B" p. 141) are framed like flats except that they have several toggle-bars (in this case called **stretchers**) and no corner-braces. The stretchers should be not more than 6′ 0″ apart. Note that the end stretchers (corresponding to the rails in a flat) carry through. **Ceiling-plates** are employed instead of profile-blocks. They facilitate dismantling and provide rings from which the ceiling may be hung. These plates are bolted to the ends of the inside stretchers, and to the ends of the long members, with stove bolts. Five holes are provided in one end of each plate for this purpose. The other end of the plate is fitted with a special bolt and a wing-nut ("C"). Each long member of the frame is made from two lengths of wood butted together and joined by being bolted to a short piece of wood known as a **fish-plate.** Another piece of wood, called a **stiffener,** is screwed to both the fish-plate and the ends of the long members.

The canvas is made up of two or three widths. The seams run across stage and should be sewed by an awning maker. The canvas must be tacked and glued to the end members, which are used as rollers when the ceiling is dismantled. It can simply be tacked to the long members.

Book ceilings ("A" p. 141) are made with profile-blocks and hinged together before canvassing.

Doors and Doorframes

A long time ago I bought a secondhand door and tried to use it on stage. It still haunts me. Stage doorframes are not rigid enough to carry even the lightest house door. Mine dragged on the floor so that every entrance and exit became an acrobatic feat. Special doors and doorframes must be built for stage use. Fortunately they are easily made and cheaper to build than to buy.

Doors. The simplest type of door is made like a flat ("F" p. 87). The corner-braces are held in place with mending-plates. The toggle-bar is of 1″ x 6″ white pine attached with corner-irons. The lock is screwed on and a hole is bored in the toggle-bar for the **spindle.** The dead-bolts on all stage locks should be removed to keep actors from locking themselves on stage by mistake. When the knobs are to be used on the other edge of the door, the first hole can be plugged and another bored on the far end of the toggle-bar. Such a door is particularly adaptable. It can be painted to represent a plank door ("B" p. 15), or molding can be applied to give a paneled effect. In fact so many treatments are possible that this type of door will answer all the needs of most groups.

The door shown at "G" p. 87 is made entirely of 1" x 6". It can be employed where a particularly realistic panel effect is desired, but its chief purpose is to permit an imitation glass panel to be used. This may be either wire screen for clear glass or muslin for frosted glass. Where a breakaway panel is needed, this type of door is essential. The panel is made of the cheap plywood used in certain types of crates, and is deeply scored on the back in a crisscross pattern with a saw so that it will break easily. It is then screwed to the back of the door. Of course, one such panel is provided for each performance.

When a door is to open onstage, it must be made like the one shown at "H," as it can be seen from both sides, and its edge must show thickness. This is of 1¼" x 1¼" (actual dimensions) white pine with a strip of 1¼" x 5" (actual dimensions) set in to carry the knobs. Note the countersinking for the hinges and the beveled edge on the knob side. A lock is not used, but knobs are provided. Since this door cannot be reversed like doors "F" and "G," it must be turned upside down if the hinges are to be brought to the other side.

The two-sided door is hard for anyone but an expert craftsman to build. I suggest having it made at a lumber mill where it will cost about $9.00. Such a door will last forever, but if the initial cost is too great, arrange to have your doors open offstage.

Doorframes ("A") are made entirely of 1" x 6" except for the sill which is 1" x 3". They are put together with 1½" x 9 screws and reinforced with corner-irons and mending-plates.

The sill must be beveled to keep the actors from tripping over it, but 3" at each end are left square to take the corner-irons that hold the sill to the jambs. Note also the notch cut in the bottom of the jambs to receive the sill iron of the flat.

The catch for the lock is attached to a piece of 1" x 6"

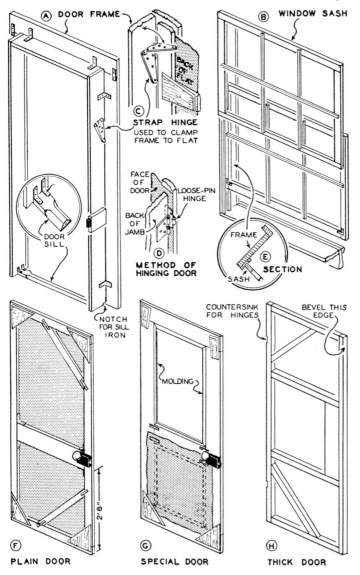

A DOOR FRAME

B WINDOW SASH

C STRAP HINGE
USED TO CLAMP
FRAME TO FLAT

BACK OF FLAT

D METHOD OF
HINGING DOOR

FACE OF DOOR

LOOSE-PIN HINGE

BACK OF JAMB

DOOR SILL

E SECTION

FRAME

SASH

NOTCH FOR SILL IRON

F PLAIN DOOR

2' 6"

G SPECIAL DOOR

MOLDING

COUNTERSINK FOR HINGES

H THICK DOOR

BEVEL THIS EDGE

screwed to the side of the jamb. This projects ¾" behind the rest of the frame.

Hinging Doors. Doors that swing offstage are hung on the back of the frame instead of inside it like the doors in a home. This simplifies the work of hinging since an exact fit is unnecessary. Loose-pin backflaps are used for hinges ("D"). One leaf is screwed to the face of the door with the bent part sticking past the edge. The other leaf is turned over so that it is in the reverse of its normal position. This leaf is screwed to the back of the door jamb. The process may seem complicated even with the help of the illustration, but it is simple enough if tried with a real hinge. One side of each hinge-leaf is countersunk for the screw heads. The other side must be placed against the wood. If this point is watched, it is impossible to make a mistake.

Time will be saved if the hinging is carried out as follows: begin by screwing the hinges to the face of the door; turn over the loose leaves; lay the frame on its face on the floor; lay the door on the frame so that it is flush at the top and on both sides; and screw the hinges to the frame. This method is very quick and automatically gives the necessary ¾" clearance at the bottom.

Doors that open onstage are more difficult to hinge. They go inside their frames and must fit with a fair degree of accuracy. They are hung on butt hinges which are screwed in the notches shown in the sketch ("H"). Note that the far edge of the door is beveled. The pin side of the hinge must be on the same face of the door as the sharp side of the bevel; otherwise the door will not close properly. A stop must be provided in the frame for the door to close against. Three strips of 1" x 2" are used for this. They run around the inside of the frame 1¼" from the face so that when the door is placed against them, it will be flush with the face of the frame. To hang a door of this type the hinges are first screwed to the edge of the door. Then both door and frame are stood upright. A piece of 1" x 3" is placed under the door to raise it off the floor and provide clearance. Lastly the hinges are screwed to the frame.

Windows

Window frames are built like doorframes except that they are the same at top and bottom instead of having a beveled sill. In fact, one frame may serve for both purposes, if the two types of sill are made interchangeable. This is indicated on p. 10 where the part of the window frame below the little arrows may be detached and replaced with a door sill.

The sash for a **casement** window is shown at "A" p. 15. White pine lumber is used. The inside stile of each sash is of 1″ x 2″. The outside stile and the rails are of 1″ x 3″, as these members overlap the frame. The joints are made with corner-plates. The diamond-shaped panes are outlined with twilled tape tacked to the back of the frame. Generally no attempt is made to imitate glass, but if this is desired, a rectangle of wire screen can be attached to the back of each sash.

A **double-hung** window is shown at "B" p. 87. The upper sash is 2″ wider than the lower, because it overlaps the frame. The lower sash must be narrower than the inside of the frame in order to slide easily. The drawing on p. 10 brings out this difference in width. It also shows that the top rail and the stiles of the upper sash are 1″ x 3″, while the lower rail is of 1″ x 2″. In the bottom sash this arrangement is reversed. Note also that in the upper sash the rails carry through. In the bottom sash this is true of the stiles. The crosspieces that outline the individual panes are merely thin strips of wood screwed to the back of the frame with ¾″ x 5 screws. They are not fitted together as in real windows but merely overlap. Lattice strips ripped in half are good for this purpose.

The lower sash slides in a groove made by nailing two strips of wood to each side of the frame ("E" p. 87). To make the window stay up when raised, two pieces of thin metal ½″ x 6″ are needed. A hole for a screw is punched near one end of each piece, which is then screwed in the bottom of the groove with its free end up. The ends are bent so they act as catches and spring out under the sash when it is raised. The pieces must be set the same height on both sides to keep the sash level. To lower the window, grasp the bottom rail from below and push back the metal catches with the thumbs. This movement will not be noticed by the audience even where there are no window draperies to hide it.

Bookcases

Bookcases are merely window frames with dummy shelves and dummy books. The frames that support the books are made entirely of 1″ x 2″ ("F" p. 91). Note that all of them, except the one at the bottom, have pieces laid flat to imitate shelves. The books are best made by ripping wallboard into strips with beveled edges. These strips are then cut into lengths corresponding to the height of the books. Stage books are larger than real ones. This process can be carried out only with a power saw. If the use of such a saw cannot be obtained, the books may be merely cut from corrugated board, although the result will be much less convincing. Care in painting books greatly increases their realism, but strong colors should be avoided. Books should be painted before they are fastened to the shelf-frames. This fastening is done with 4d common nails. The nails project at the back and may easily be knocked out again when it is necessary to rearrange the "library." The bookcase may be backed by covering it with painted canvas, with a black drapery, or simply by placing a flat behind it.

Fireplaces

There are so many kinds of fireplaces that it is impossible to describe all the methods used to make them. The one illustrated at "A" and "B" p. 91 should, however, serve as an example of the basic principle on which most of them are constructed. These drawings were made from a point slightly below the fireplace in order to bring out the construction.

As shown at "A," two frames, like small flats, are made. These are joined by **spreaders**. Diagonal braces may be inserted when necessary. This whole framework is held to-

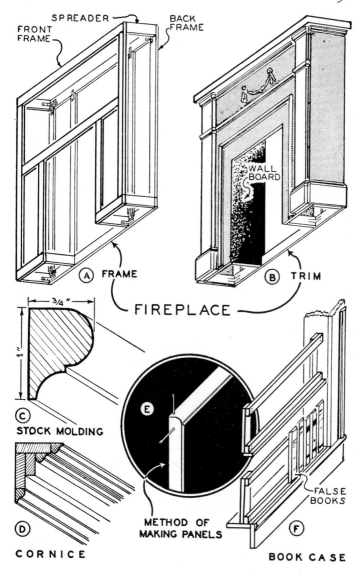

SPREADER

FRONT FRAME

BACK FRAME

Ⓐ FRAME

WALL BOARD

Ⓑ TRIM

FIREPLACE

3/4"

1"

Ⓒ STOCK MOLDING

Ⓓ CORNICE

Ⓔ

METHOD OF MAKING PANELS

FALSE BOOKS

Ⓕ

BOOK CASE

gether by mending-plates and corner-irons. The outside is canvassed, but wallboard lines the sides of the opening.

Practically all types of fireplaces are built on similar frameworks. "B" shows a formal variety obtained by decorating "A" with 1″ x 6″ molding, and an ornament made from real rope sewed to the canvas. Stone fireplaces are more complicated. They must first be covered with chicken wire, then with wadded paper or rags and finally have a layer of wrinkled canvas sewed on top to simulate the surface of the stone.

Trim

Many other scene-units besides fireplaces are dependent for their effectiveness on trim. Detail less than ½″ in thickness may be merely painted, especially if it is on the back wall, but deeper relief must be actually built. This work is slow, but pays big dividends in the finish it gives to scenery.

Molding of the type illustrated at "C" p. 91 will answer every stage purpose. "F" on the same page shows how it can be used to trim a door, window, or bookcase frame. "B" gives a more elaborate treatment, common on fireplaces. Plain doors can be turned into paneled doors like those on p. 10 by making rectangles of molding and nailing them to the face of the door. The method of constructing these panels is illustrated at "E." The joints are mitered and held together with 4d finishing nails placed as shown. Panels built in this way are surprisingly strong, and may be taken off the door and kept for future use. Paneled walls may be imitated by the same process, but they introduce so many complications into scene shifts that the beginner should use them only for one-set shows.

The panels may be attached to the set by driving tacks into them from the back through the canvas. This method is not recommended, however, because the panels have a tendency to flap when an actor closes a door. A better way is to insert additional wooden members (usually toggle-bars or corner-braces) in the back of the scene-unit and hold them in place with mending-plates. This provides a firm base to which the panels can be fastened with 4d finishing nails. These extra members are also used to carry other sorts of decoration such as pictures and light-brackets which are too heavy to be supported by the canvas itself.

"D" shows how a cornice can be made up from 1″ x 2″, 1″ x 3″, and molding. Straight runs are easy, but the reader should note that molding which does much zigzagging (see the upper one on the fireplace at "B") makes a tedious job.

Papier-mâché provides an easy way to make trim, if there is a surface of solid wood on which it can be molded. To make *papier-mâché,* tear up old newspapers, cover the scraps with water and let them soak overnight. Then squeeze out most of the water and pour in paste that has already been mixed. Now drive 4d common nails into the background so that their projecting heads will form a reinforcement for the *papier-mâché.* The substance itself can then be applied. It is best put on in thin layers; otherwise the paste may spoil before it dries.

Perhaps the most common use for *papier-mâché* arises from its ability to imitate curved moldings. Near at hand the work looks very crude, but at a distance it is most effective, especially if its outlines are strengthened by paint.

Platforms

The platform, an underneath view of which is shown at "A" p. 95, is the simplest of all scene-units to build. The top is simply three 2″ x 4″s set on edge, with boards (which may be anything from 1″ x 6″ to 1″ x 12″) nailed across them with 8d nails. Even if a very large platform is desired, it is well to make it up in sections, which should rarely be more than 5′ 0″ wide or 10′ 0″ long. The width is fixed by the fact that 1″ boards will not safely span a gap of more than 2′ 6″.

Legs. The legs of the platforms are of 2″ x 4″ and bolt on with ⅜″ x 4″ carriage bolts ("B"). Notice that the legs are not in the extreme corners, but are kept back 1⅝″ to make room for the 2″ x 4″ cross member that supports the central beam of the top. Platforms over 7′ 0″ long require an extra pair of legs in the middle with an additional cross member as well. Cross members are bolted to the top of the legs with $\frac{3}{8}''$ x 6" carriage bolts. Platforms built in this way are not rigid without the diagonal braces, two to a leg, that are shown in the sketch. These are made of scrap lumber nailed in place with 6d or 8d nails.

Padding. All platform tops must be padded to prevent noise. Whether rug padding or cotton batting is used, it must be covered with canvas or burlap. For platforms supposed to represent wood or cut stone it is desirable to have the edges squarer than they can be made by simply pulling the canvas over the edge of the padding and tacking it down. In this case strips of wood $\frac{3}{4}''$ wide and $\frac{1}{4}''$ thick can be run around the top of the platform flush with the edge.

Cotton padding may be kept in place by sticking 8 oz. tacks in small squares of cardboard and driving them through the padding and into the platform floor at intervals of one or two feet. This must be done before the padding is covered with canvas. If it is done afterward we will get an "upholstery" effect which is most undesirable.

Cover-flats, as the pieces used to mask the exposed sides of platforms are called, need differ only in size from regular flats. When they are built special, they are made with screws instead of clout nails and mending-plates instead of profile-blocks. Often pieces of wallboard can be substituted for cover-flats.

Stairs

A set of stairs (viewed from below to show their construction) is shown at "D" p. 95. The **carriages,** as the saw-shaped pieces that carry the treads are called, must be laid out with care. The method is simple enough but the top and bottom steps are not the same size as the others and it is easy to make a mistake. "F" shows how a steel square is used to mark a carriage for standard 7" risers and 10" treads. The 7" mark on one leg of the square and the 10" mark on the other are placed on one edge of the board. A pencil line drawn against

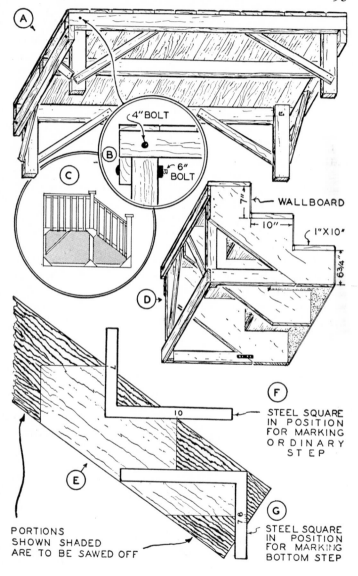

A

4" BOLT

B

6" BOLT

C

D

WALLBOARD

7"

10"

1"X10"

6¾"

F

STEEL SQUARE
IN POSITION
FOR MARKING
ORDINARY
STEP

10

E

G

STEEL SQUARE
IN POSITION
FOR MARKING
BOTTOM STEP

7 6

PORTIONS
SHOWN SHADED
ARE TO BE SAWED OFF

the square will then give the shape of the step. Steps of any proportions can be laid out in this way by using the right dimensions on the square. After the first step is outlined the square is moved so that the 10″ point comes where the 7″ point was before, and the second step can be marked.

The bottom step of the carriage must allow for the thickness of the board used as a tread. This is almost always ¾″, so the bottom riser of the carriage is made 6¼″ high ("G"). In the same way the top tread is ¾″ narrower than the other treads, to make room for the piece of 1″ x 2″ that runs across the back of the top step just under the tread.

Yellow pine is generally used for stairs. The carriages should be cut from 1″ x 12″. Treads may be 1″ x 10″. The uprights are 1″ x 3″ and the cross braces 1″ x 2″. For rigidity the carriages should not be placed more than 2′ 0″ apart. A spacing of 2′ 6″ is an absolute maximum. The other elements of the framework are shown in the drawing. If the sides of the stairs are to appear solid they may be covered with canvas. When this is to be done, a piece of 1″ x 2″ must be nailed to the side of the upright leg and fitted neatly between the top of the horizontal member and the bottom of the side carriage. This brings the side of the leg flush with the other two members and permits the canvas to fit smoothly.

If the steps are to be padded (and for most purposes they should be to eliminate noise) the padding is applied like that used for platform tops. Where the steps are supposed to be stone or to simulate rock forms ("B" p. 33), no edging of wooden strips is necessary. With supposedly wooden steps, however, the edging strips must be used. Their height should be deducted from that of the bottom carriage-riser so that the height of the finished step will be exactly 7″.

The risers of the steps themselves are made of wallboard nailed in place with 4d common nails. Each riser should stop about ⅛″ below the level of the step; otherwise the actors may scuff it off when they walk downstairs.

Where the stairs are made to represent finished woodwork it is well to provide a **nosing**, as the little overhang of the tread seen in houses is called. Stock molding applied over the wallboard of the riser does nicely for this, provided it is held in place with 8d finishing nails.

Stair Rails. While the sides of the stairs themselves are often canvassed, any sort of balustrade should be made as a separate unit. Such a unit usually rests on the floor and includes a sort of flat to cover the sides of the steps and any platform involved. The inset "C" p. 95 shows an example of this type of unit.

Irregular Forms

Although smooth curves are difficult to make on stage, irregular objects such as tree trunks and rocks are quite simple, thanks to the special qualities of poultry netting.

Tree trunks are constructed as shown at "G" p. 99. The frame is made entirely of 1″ x 3″. There are four uprights and four pairs of cross braces. The sizes of the cross braces determine the size and shape of the tree. The bottom pair of braces is the largest while the others are progressively smaller. The three upper pairs are merely bolted together, but the bottom pair has extra pieces screwed underneath the ends of the top member to make a level surface on which the tree will rest.

The cross braces are attached to the uprights with tight-pin backflaps. These hinges are merely an easy way of making an otherwise difficult joint. They do not permit the finished tree to fold up.

The frame is covered with poultry netting, which is attached to the wood with poultry netting staples. Where two pieces of netting meet, they are tied with stovepipe wire. The netting may be pulled about a good deal without losing its strength and thus can be made to fit almost any rough shape. If further irregularities are desired, loose bundles of rags or paper can be attached to the outside of the netting.

The bark of the tree is made of canvas, sewed to the netting with stout linen thread. A curved upholsterer's needle is necessary for this work. The canvas may be sewed flat or may be wrinkled into vertical folds. The creases must be irregular or the result will look more like a crude column than a tree.

Elaborate tree forms can be built on this plan, including those with branching tops. They require more complicated frames and it is sometimes desirable to bolt the members together rather than to follow the hinging method shown in the sketch. **Tree stumps** must be strong enough to permit an actor to sit or stand on them. This calls for a strong frame and a top of 1″ boards.

Rocks that do not have to bear weight are made like trees. The framework for such rocks is usually extremely simple since it does not need to be very strong. If the rocks are bent out of shape during a shift, no harm is done. For elaborate platform scenes, cover-flats made of poultry netting rocks will give a splendid effect with little trouble.

Repairs

It is usually an easy matter to mend broken scenery. If a wooden member breaks, a mending-plate, a wooden fish-plate, or a mending-batten can be screwed over the crack. Even a flat with a broken stile can be fixed in this way and used for a year or two afterward.

Damaged canvas can be repaired still more simply. A tear is patched by pasting or gluing a square of canvas in back of the break. It takes two people to do this properly; one holds a board in front to provide a smooth surface and the other plasters the patch on from the rear. If the work is well done, the damage will not show from the front after it has been painted over. Canvas that has acquired bulges due to contact with a stagehand's shoulder, or other round object, will stretch tight again if water is spattered (p. 110) on its back. Canvas shrinks easily, so a very little water does the trick.

Flameproofing

Some states have laws requiring all scenery to be treated with so-called flameproofing liquids. From a practical point of view, the process is not worth the trouble. Painted canvas does not burn easily anyway, and the flameproofing solutions

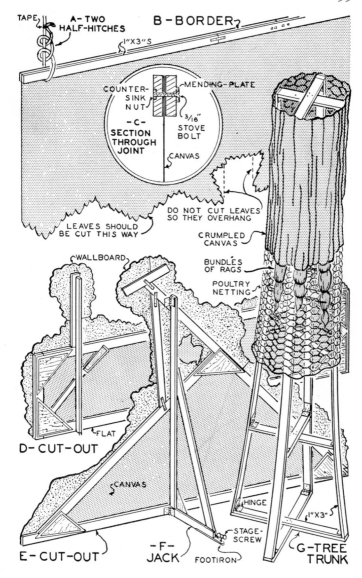

TAPE
A- TWO HALF-HITCHES

B - BORDER

1"X3"S

COUNTER-SINK NUT
MENDING-PLATE
-C- SECTION THROUGH JOINT
3/16" STOVE BOLT
CANVAS

LEAVES SHOULD BE CUT THIS WAY

DO NOT CUT LEAVES SO THEY OVERHANG

CRUMPLED CANVAS

BUNDLES OF RAGS

POULTRY NETTING

WALLBOARD

FLAT

D- CUT-OUT

CANVAS

HINGE

E- CUT-OUT

-F- JACK

STAGE-SCREW

FOOTIRON

1"X3"

G-TREE TRUNK

used on wood are completely ineffective. When I was a student at the Yale Drama School, I used to take scraps of "flameproofed" wood home to use for kindling and found them well suited to the purpose.

If the laws in your state require flameproofing, flameproofed canvas must be used, and the woodwork of all scenery will have to be treated by whatever process the fire inspectors recommend. The wood must be treated before canvassing, as most flameproofing liquids will make white stains on any paint that is used over them even after they are dry. No amateur should attempt to flameproof canvas himself.

CHAPTER VIII

SCENE PAINTING

Old-fashioned scene painting required a tremendous amount of knowledge and skill. No amateur, even if he were a first class artist in his own right, could hope to turn out a satisfactory job. Fortunately, simpler techniques have been evolved. They are so easy that one fairly experienced painter can run a crew of six or eight completely green hands and still turn out a perfect set.

Scene Paint

The scene painter uses a water-color paint similar to kalsomine, but instead of buying this already prepared he mixes it himself. The ingredients are paint in powder form known as **dry color,** water, and **size.**

Mixing Pigments. Scene paints are too cheap to be either chemically or chromatically pure, so even the most experienced artist needs to make preliminary experiments before actually mixing a bucketful of paint. These experiments can be carried out on a clean piece of white pine. Dip a finger in a color and shake off the paint on the board. Repeat with another color and then mix the two together with the finger. If other colors are needed they may be added, but it is rare that more than four are mixed together. Black should seldom be used in such combinations.

This test mixing is important, for if colors are blended in a pail, the resulting hue will be first too dark and then too light, until what started out to be a half bucket of paint grows to be two buckets. Even the experienced painter cannot entirely avoid waste of this sort, and the beginner may expect to throw a quarter of his paint away for one reason or another.

Pigments should be mixed dry. Wet paint is almost always darker than dry paint, particularly in the lighter shades. Unfortunately, even when dry the color is never exactly the same as the finished tone, and no amateur ever gains enough experience to mix colors with certainty. On the other hand, scene paint is the most flexible of all artistic media, and if the first coat is too dark, the difficulty can usually be corrected by making the next one lighter.

Size serves as a binder and keeps the paint from rubbing off. It may be of several kinds, but the best is a sort of thin glue. The glue is bought dry (see p. 106). To prepare size, fill a pail two-thirds full of glue, add enough water to cover the glue, and allow to stand overnight. The next day pour a few inches of water in another pail. Put the glue pail in this, making a double-boiler, and place the combination on a stove. Care must be taken not to have the fire too hot, and to see that the water in the bottom pail does not boil away. After some twenty minutes the glue will assume a uniform consistency equal to that of molasses. In this state it is known as size and is ready for use. It hardens when cold but may be re-melted as often as desired.

Size will keep indefinitely but spoils rapidly when mixed with paint. After a few days, the mixed paint acquires a putrid odor that spreads to the farthest corners of the theater. If mixed paint must be kept for some time, a 20% solution of carbolic acid may be added as a preservative. One tablespoonful to the pail is all that should be used, as the acid may affect the color of the paint.

Preparing Paint. After the size is made and melted and the colors are blended, the actual preparation of the paint is extremely simple. The pigments are usually mixed in the pail which is to contain the finished paint. Water is added and stirred in with a stick until all the powdered color is dissolved. The experienced painter learns to judge the consistency by eye, but the novice will do well to test his paint on a bare piece of canvas. When enough water has been added, the paint will spread evenly but will not be thick enough to clog the weave of the material. Most beginners mix paint too thick. This is not only wasteful but slows down the work as thick paint is difficult to apply.

A good plan is to prepare only half the dry pigment at once. Then if the first batch is too thin more powder can be added. The dry paint will also serve as a sample if it becomes necessary to mix more.

After the dry color and the water have been mixed, the size can be poured in. The usual rule is two or three cupfuls of size to the 12-quart pail of paint, but the amount varies with the exact thickness of the size. One test is to pour in size until the paint feels slippery when rubbed between the thumb and index finger. A surer test is to daub some of the mixture on a piece of canvas and let it dry. If the color rubs off, more size is required. If the glue appears on the surface in tiny drops, too much has been used.

Painter's Equipment

Even in small groups, where the same people both build and paint the scenery, it is customary to keep the paints, brushes, etc., in a separate place called the **paint shop.** The paint shop may be only a corner of the stage or it may even be only a corner of a cupboard, but it should be sacred to painting, and hammers and nails should not be left there.

Brushes are the most expensive part of the painter's equipment. Professional painters tend to use a large number of types and sizes, but amateurs will do well to standardize on the three types shown in the cuts on p. 111. The most important of these is the **laying-in** brush illustrated at "A" and "E." You can pay fancy prices for these, but an ordinary house painter's 4″ **wall brush** with 4″ bristles can be bought for $2.75 and serves nicely. Make sure to get a **solid-bristle** brush, as the cheaper variety holds so little paint that it doubles the work. The equipment should include one brush of this type for each painter.

For painting details such as leaves, stones, bricks, etc., the **foliage brush** illustrated in "C" is satisfactory. (Paint stores call this a **chiseled sash tool.**) The No. 8 size is the best. It sells for 40¢. Two or three of these will meet the needs of most theaters.

Fine work such as **lining** ("D") is done with the **angular liner** illustrated. This brush comes in several styles, but all are characterized by the fact that the ends of the bristles are cut off on a slant. The ½" (45¢ each) and ¾" (60¢ each) sizes are the most useful. Only one brush of this kind is required unless the painting is to be very elaborate.

Pails. Twelve-quart galvanized iron pails (30¢ each), sauce pans, lard pails, etc., are used to hold mixed paint. I cannot say how many to get because no paint crew ever had enough. Five buckets (two for the glue-size) are probably a minimum, while a dozen would be average. Buy only the best quality buckets as cheap ones soon rust.

Miscellaneous Equipment. A two- or three-burner gas stove is needed to heat the size. If gas is not available, a kerosene stove may be substituted.

A sink with running water (plus a plumber's **force pump** to clean it out when it gets stopped up) is almost essential.

Paint **bins,** one for each color, save time and help to keep the shop in some sort of order. These may be anything from a row of wooden boxes lined with building paper, to neatly built affairs with self-closing lids. Each bin should be provided with a scoop (10¢ each) as dipping out paint with the fingers is messy business.

Another important painting accessory is a rolling platform called a **boomerang** (p. 121) from which the upper part of the scenery can be painted. This should be about 2' 4" wide, 10' 0" long and 6' 0" high, with ladders at each end for easy access. Such a platform can be built of yellow pine for about $7.00, including 4" rubber-tired casters.

The painter's equipment should also include a number of yardsticks and **stirring paddles** (both given away at the paint store) and a ball of stout cotton cord.

Pigments and Supplies

The dry color used by the scene painter may be purchased at most paint stores and some hardware stores. In cities of medium size it is usual for only one or two shops to carry a full line. In small towns the colors may have to be ordered. Ready-mixed kalsomine is sometimes substituted for dry color, but it is unsatisfactory and expensive. Furthermore it is hard to find except in pastel shades.

During the past ten years, I have slowly evolved a basic palette from which I now depart only on rare occasions. It includes the following pigments:

Whiting (5¢ lb.) should be bought in 50-lb. or 100-lb. sacks or drums. A single set of scenery may require 50 lbs.

Drop Black (30¢ lb.) a good black but not always available. **Hercules Black** may be substituted. If your color man tries to sell you something else, make sure that it will dissolve easily in water. **Lamp Black** is the black most widely sold, but it takes half a day to dissolve a pound of it.

Yellow Ocher (8¢ lb.) the better grades of which are sometimes called **French Ocher.** A fair quality of this is desirable since the cheaper varieties are muddy.

Venetian Red (6¢ lb.) a brownish red. Notice how much difference in consistency there is between this pigment and the colors already mentioned.

Burnt Umber (10¢ lb.) a dark brown. Mixed with Venetian Red this makes a cheap and satisfactory substitute for **Burnt Sienna** which would otherwise be an essential pigment.

Permanent Red (40¢ lb.) a difficult color to work with, but its cheapness compared with other bright reds gives it a place.

Chrome Yellow, Medium (20¢ lb.) so little used that it may be omitted from the stock colors and bought only as needed. **Chrome Yellow, Light,** may be substituted.

Chrome Green, Medium (15¢ lb.) the cheapest of the reasonably bright greens. Cost is important, as a good deal of green will be used.

Ultramarine (40¢ lb.) a fairly satisfactory blue, but its principal virtue is its low cost, compared to other blue pigments.

As you can see, colors vary widely in price. The difference is even greater than appears, for the more expensive colors are heavier and will cover fewer square feet per pound. Nor does the difference in pigments stop with their cost. Of all the colors listed, only Venetian Red and Burnt Umber seem closely allied. Whiting is fluffy and does not go far. Yellow Ocher is lumpy, so that mixtures in which it is used always turn out yellower than one expects. Prepared Permanent Red cannot be kept overnight, as the red settles to the bottom in a hard cake. Each pigment has its idiosyncrasies which only experience will teach, but none of them are so freakish that the beginner cannot use them effectively at the first try even if the resulting color is not always exactly what he expects.

Glue may be bought at a hardware or paint store. The cake and flake varieties are better than the granulated. A fair grade costs 25¢ per pound. It takes about ten pounds to paint a set.

Chalk. If the scenery does not have to be handled, stick chalk can be used for putting on finishing touches. Both white and colored chalk can be bought in boxes at five-and-ten-cent stores. Some brands of colored chalk are more vivid than others and it is well to examine different stocks to find the best. Stationers carry a very brilliant chalk, but it is correspondingly expensive. Mason's chalk, which comes in lumps at 5¢ each, is also used (p. 119).

Charcoal, of the stick type used by artists, may be employed where small shadows and other dark accents are needed on the finished set. The softest grade is the best. Charcoal is often used to sketch in designs to be painted, but for this purpose **copying pencils** (usually known as **indelible pencils**) may be preferred. The pencils may be bought at any stationer's. Their advantage consists in the fact that they will show through several layers of paint, so outlines drawn with them will not be covered by the first coat. Only a light line should be made; otherwise the pencil will stain the paint purple.

Color Mixing

Although most scenery can be painted satisfactorily with no more knowledge of color than such elementary facts as that yellow and blue make green, blue and red make violet, and red and yellow make orange, nevertheless some acquaintance with color-theory makes the work much easier. Everyone interested in mixing pigments should read *The Painter's Terms* by Arthur Pope, Harvard University Press, Cambridge 1929, which contains everything one needs to know on the subject. A bare outline is all that can be included here.

There are only three ways in which **tones** (colors, including black, white and gray) can vary. The most obvious of these is **hue.** For instance, one tone can be red, another orange, and a third green. The second type of variation is in **intensity.** Thus gray-blue is lower in intensity than bright blue, and tan is a low-intensity orange. All the brownish tones are low-intensity variations of yellow or orange, a fact which the beginner sometimes finds hard to realize.

"A" p. 109 shows the principal hues arranged in a circle. These hues are at a theoretical full intensity which no real pigment can ever reach. The neutral point in the center of the circle may be regarded as of zero intensity. The approximate location of our stock pigments is also shown. Whiting and Drop Black may be considered as neutral.

This color-circle symbolizes a theory, but it has a practical value as well. If we draw a straight line joining any two pigments in the chart we will find that the result of any mixture of these two colors will fall along that line. Thus if we mix Chrome Yellow and Venetian Red we will get a medium-intensity orange, while Permanent Red and Ultramarine will give a low-intensity violet. Even a glance at the chart shows that bright orange and bright violet can not be obtained by mixing any pigments in our stock list.

The third way in which tones may vary is called **value.** Black is the lowest value, white the highest, and all the other tones fall in between. In an ordinary photograph all the variation consists of value-differences. The approximate values of our stock pigments are shown at "B."

If we wish to mix a light tone of a certain hue we can add Whiting to the appropriate pigment. Thus pale blue can be made by adding Whiting to Ultramarine. The fact that Whiting is a neutral in chart "A" should warn us that our pale blue will not be as intense as our Ultramarine was. This **graying** effect is increased by the cheap pigments used for scene paint.

Unfortunately black is unsatisfactory in practice for lowering the value of colors. For this purpose we must resort to using Burnt Umber, balanced if necessary with a little Ultramarine.

Painting Techniques

There are innumerable methods of applying paint to canvas, but only those described here are used for general purposes. The reader should learn at least the name of each process and the effect it produces before proceeding further. How these processes are employed to imitate leaves, brick, wallpaper, etc. will be discussed later.

Flat Coat. The simplest method of applying paint is to brush it on smoothly so as to produce an even tone over the whole area. If the surface has not been previously painted, all that is necessary is to avoid letting the brush strokes run in the same direction. Many beginners try to keep all their strokes parallel because this is the proper technique for applying oil paint to wood. In scenic work, however, it is definitely a mistake as it tends to produce a pattern. Strokes should be made in all directions at random.

If the surface has been painted before, additional precautions must be taken to prevent the undercoat from **working through.** The old paint is held in place by the size it contains. The water in the new coat dissolves this size and permits the two colors to mix. In order to avoid this, the fresh paint should be applied quickly and with as little brushing as possible. When the old paint is dampened, the friction of the brush rubs it off and mixes it with the new. If this does happen, it cannot be corrected by applying more paint while the surface is wet. Let it dry and give it another coat if necessary, but any attempt to patch up a bad job while it is still wet is certain to make matters worse. A flat coat put on over a previously painted area is almost always splotchy, particularly if the new

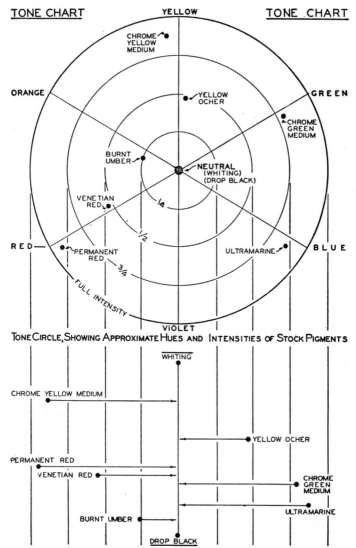

TONE CHART
TONE CHART

Tone Circle, Showing Approximate Hues and Intensities of Stock Pigments

Diagram Showing Approximate Relative Values of Stock Pigments

coat is lighter than the old one. This is usually unimportant unless the difference in tone is marked.

A painter can paint from the floor level up to a height of about 6′ 0″, so it takes two **flights** to cover a 12′ 0″ set. Work on the upper flight may be done from ladders, but this is a hard and thankless job. A boomerang makes the second flight as easy as the first.

Spatter. When an area is stippled with small spots of paint each about ¼″ in diameter, the process is called **spattering** ("A" p. 111). The ability to spatter well may be quickly learned, but it is important to follow directions closely. Stand with the left side toward the surface to be painted. Dip the brush in the paint and then wipe off most of it on the side of the bucket. As proficiency is gained, more paint can be left on the brush, but in the beginning it should be fairly dry. Experts stand less than a yard away from the work, but the beginner is advised to stand nearly twice this far for the first trial. Hold the brush in the right hand with the handle horizontal and the bristles parallel to the work. The left hand is held with its back to the work and with the fingers pointing downward. Strike the brush against the palm of the left hand and a shower of paint drops will be thrown against the work. In good spattering, all the spots are about the same size. Large splashes must be avoided.

The beginner should practice single strokes at waist level until he acquires the proper knack, but in actual painting the strokes follow each other in quick succession. In fact, fast spattering is much easier than slow, because the bristles themselves have a sort of rapid rhythmic beat like a spring pendulum. If the strokes are in time with this beat, very little effort is required to keep the bristles moving. Slow spattering not only demands more labor from the right hand but greatly increases the force with which the left hand must be struck.

In practice, it is wise to start with a light spatter coat over the whole area, and then build up successive coats until the desired shade is obtained. This gives the first coat time to dry and also enables the painter to pay especial attention on the second coat to the places he missed on the first. Few people

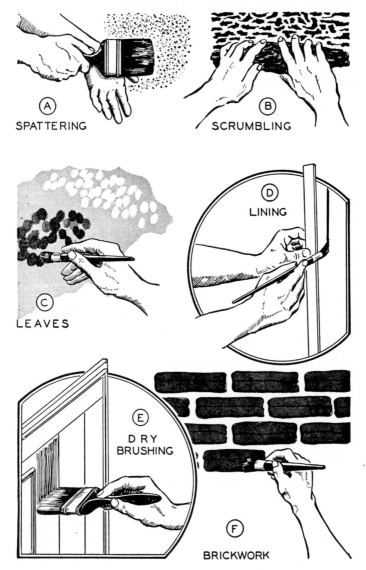

A SPATTERING

B SCRUMBLING

C LEAVES

D LINING

E DRY BRUSHING

F BRICKWORK

can spatter quite evenly and the later rounds are largely a matter of catching the bad spots. If some places are spattered too heavily, they can be corrected by re-spattering with the base color.

The beginner usually finds that the constant beating of the brush against the palm of the left hand is painful. Gloves help, and some girls like to spatter by wrapping rags around a short stick and holding this in their left hand. *Never spatter with one hand.* This makes unattractive patterns which no amount of over-spattering will correct.

Scrumbling ("B") is done by wetting a rag with paint, crumpling it into a loose wad and rolling it over the surface to be painted. The effect is somewhat like spatter, but has a definite pattern comparable to that of rough plaster. Numerous patterns are possible depending on the weave of the cloth, the way it is creased, and the amount of paint it holds. The exact process of rolling is also a factor and no two painters can achieve quite the same result. Sometimes the scrumbling is done with a light tone over a dark base and sometimes the darker tone is used for the scrumble coat. The reader will have to experiment to learn which he prefers in a particular case.

Sponging produces much the same effect as scrumbling. A coarse sponge is used instead of a cloth. The sponge may be rolled, but more characteristic patterns are produced either by patting or by various combinations of a pat and a smear. The last process is used to imitate troweled plaster or stucco.

Dry Brushing ("E"). Entirely different effects from those just mentioned may be obtained by using an almost dry laying-in brush. The tip of the brush is drawn lightly over the surface to be painted so that each bristle makes a fine line. If good results are to be obtained, the brush must be kept at right angles to the work. This process is chiefly used to imitate the grain in wood.

Theory of Scene Painting

The scene painter works for an audience whose nearest member is usually thirty feet away. Only broad effects can be plainly seen. This does not mean that all painting should be broad. On the contrary there is a whole range of effects below the clear-visibility level that are used to deceive the distant eye. It is within this range that the techniques described in the last few sections have their usefulness.

The surface of most scenery is marred by many imperfections: strippers never completely hide the joints between flats; the flats themselves are usually patched; and if the scenery has been shifted often, the paint is scuffed and scarred. When a set is painted with a single flat coat all these flaws stand out; also the set itself appears dull and lifeless. However, if the set is painted in many small areas each differing slightly from the others in color, a more interesting effect is produced, and at the same time the defects are made invisible to the audience by a type of *camouflage*. This is so true that it is a standing theatrical rule that no matter what condition a piece of scenery is in, it can be made presentable by **breaking it up** into small areas. A battered sky drop, for instance, may look like a stained piece of canvas in an exterior set, but behind a row of windows all its faults disappear and it seems like limitless space. Similarly a badly marred interior set can be disguised by dressing it with furniture, pictures, windows, curtains, etc. Tall secretaries and grandfather's clocks are especially good for this purpose. The flaws need not be covered. The fact that there is no large bare space against which they may be contrasted makes them almost invisible under the ordinary conditions of stage lighting.

The old-fashioned "scenic artist" took advantage of this principle by making his sets as fancy as possible. Each wall was paneled, and every panel was shaded until no square foot of surface was exactly the same tone as its neighbor. This does not mean that one area was red and the next yellow. Usually the variations were so slight that they were not noticed by the untrained eye, but they were there and they served their purpose.

The present day painter usually wants his walls to appear as monochrome. If he actually paints them that way he is inviting failure. No one can repeal the laws of optics. Fortunately, he can still employ the broken color teachnique of his predecessor by making the area of each tone so small and the contrasts so slight that they are below the clear-vision level of the audience. The illustrations in this book furnish an example of this. Most of them contain tones which the observer accepts as gray. Actually these tones are made up of tiny black dots. The gray exists only in the imagination. For color printing, the method is the same but here a new optical principle comes in. If red and blue inks are mixed by the printer they make a *dull* violet, but if a number of red and blue spots are printed close together the eye mixes them to a *bright* violet. The printer can thus produce more brilliant colors than the artist; in fact, he must make special efforts to soften his colors if he wants to reproduce the original. This accounts for the lurid tones seen in moving pictures and cheap postcards.

There are several ways in which the scene painter can make use of this tendency of the eye to blend small spots into a smooth tone. If he needs lively hues he can achieve them by successive spatters of properly selected colors. Chrome Yellow spattered with Permanent Red will produce a much more intense color than if the two pigments were mixed in a bucket and applied as one coat. This method will even produce a "vivid" gray if bright red and bright green are spattered over one another on a neutral background. More often the painter is interested in blending tones on his sets. By using the spatter technique the beginner can produce a smoother blend than the expert could make in any other way.

Scrumbling, sponging, and dry-brushing act on the same principle as spattering. With these, however, the eye is conscious of a vague pattern even at a distance. This pattern may be interpreted either as grain or as some kind of texture, depending on the pattern itself and the surfaces with which it is associated.

Painting Procedure

We are now ready to consider the actual painting of a set. As most scenes are interiors and most interiors call for smooth walls of (apparently) one color, let us make ours a soft leaf green. For this we shall want a flat coat and two spatter coats. Although the flat coat is essential, it serves only as a base and will be barely visible through the two spatter coats. Under these circumstances we may make it a dull yellowish green somewhat lower in value than we want the finished effect. For this we use Yellow Ocher, Chrome Green, Burnt Umber, and Whiting. The Yellow Ocher and Chrome Green produce the desired hue while the addition of Burnt Umber and Whiting diminishes the intensity without noticeably changing the value. A little extra green will be required to overcome the orange effect of the Burnt Umber. After experimenting with small quantities on a board, we mix a bucket and a half of the required dry color. This will make between two and three buckets of prepared paint and will be enough to cover our whole set. If the canvas has never been painted before, half again this amount of paint should be mixed, as new canvas is harder to cover.

The first spatter coat will be a dull bluish green slightly darker than the finished wall. We mix Chrome Green, Ultramarine, and Whiting (with, perhaps, a little Burnt Umber or Venetian Red added to lower the intensity). Three-quarters of a bucket of powder will be enough for this coat. The spatter should be applied until about as much of the background is covered as shows through. In this way the flat coat and the first spatter coat will effect the final result equally.

The second spatter coat may be mixed from the same pigments as the first, using different proportions. It should be almost the color desired for the final effect, but somewhat more intense to compensate for the dullness of the under coats. A bucket, or perhaps more, of dry color will be needed. The last coat should be quite heavy so that the earlier coats are almost invisible from a short distance.

Corrections. Scene paint rarely dries exactly the right color, but this can be taken care of in future coats. In the preceding example, for instance, suppose the flat coat had dried out a lighter and more yellowish tone than we intended. This could have been rectified by making the first spatter coat darker and bluer than we had planned. If the effect produced by the first spatter coat turned out too drab, the second spatter could have been made somewhat brighter than the original scheme called for. If the second spatter coat does not produce the effect desired we can still make corrections by applying a third spatter coat. For example, if the second spatter is not bright enough, the third spatter coat might be Chrome Green mixed with more than the usual amount of water and applied very lightly.

Almost any amount of correction can be carried out in this way. A thorough knowledge of color is required to take full advantage of the various situations that arise, but anyone with a little experience in paint-mixing should be able to produce good results.

Blending. Often a set is painted by blending two or more colors together. One way to do this is to mix the colors in the first coat. Suppose we want to produce a mottled effect of pink, cream, and pale blue, for the heavenly courtroom in *Liliom.* The paints are mixed and kept beside the painter while he works. A patch of pink is painted with a patch of cream on one side and a patch of blue on the other. The colors are blended on the canvas while wet. A separate brush is used for each color and the painter usually works with a brush in each hand.

A similar technique will produce a splendid imitation of marble. The flat coat is put on, and while it is still wet the veins are worked in with an angular liner.

If the effect desired is not merely an irregular mixture of colors, but a smooth, even blend, a spatter technique is simpler and can be more easily controlled. Suppose we want to blend a wall from yellow at the bottom to green at the top. The flat coat may be a dull yellowish green. The bottom is then spattered with yellow and the top with green. The yellow is carried a foot or two into the green area and *vice versa,* letting each color fade away by using a very light spatter at the edge.

Texture. So far we have been speaking of walls that are intended to seem as smooth as possible. Often, however, we desire an appearance of texture. Sometimes this texture imitates a real condition such as rough plaster. At other times all that is desired is an abstract "depth" which is difficult to describe but easy to recognize if once seen. This latter effect is gained by the use of spatter. The spatter is applied just as it would be on a smooth wall, but instead of using tones that are nearly alike, the colors mixed for the various coats differ more or less widely. For our dull green wall, for instance, we could have substituted a first coat of yellowish brown (Yellow Ocher and Burnt Umber). The second coat might have been light blue (Ultramarine and Whiting). The same final spatter coat would have been used. Such a process would have produced walls of almost the same tone as those painted by the first method, but instead of seeming smooth they would have appeared to have this mysterious quality of "depth."

The methods used to imitate natural textures vary with the results desired. Usually they call for some sort of scrumbling or sponging, with perhaps a spatter coat before or after. A cream-colored wall of rough plaster, for instance, might have a flat coat of light blue, spattered with a slightly darker violet. Over this we could put a scrumble coat of cream-colored paint. If a rougher finish were desired, we might add a light spatter of still deeper violet dulled somewhat with a little Burnt Umber.

Shadows. In the old-fashioned theater, the lighting was made as shadowless as possible, so any shadows that were supposed to be cast on the set had to be painted in. With good modern lighting most of the shadows are actually cast. Nevertheless it is well to reinforce them with paint. One example of this occurs in connection with molding, which should be both shadowed and high-lighted whether or not the stage lights strike it from a natural angle.

Since the actors occupy only the lower part of a set, it is customary to shadow the upper part to make it less interesting and therefore less likely to attract the attention of the audience. This shadowing is much more important than it may seem and represents one of the striking differences between the usual amateur set and its professional counterpart. The shadow may be produced by spattering the upper third of the set with either a darker tone of the set color or with a deep purplish paint made by mixing Ultramarine and Burnt Umber. The shadow is very dark at the top of the walls but thins out eight or nine feet from the floor so that its bottom edge blends with the main tone of the set. For the best results the shadow is brought a little lower in the corners than in the center of the walls.

Woodwork is imitated on stage by graining the surface with an almost dry brush ("E" p. 111). If a special type of wood is to be copied, a sample should be studied and the colors matched as closely as possible. The nature of the stroke is also important. Some woods have even, regular, grains that call for long, almost straight, brush strokes. Others have irregular grains that require short, wavy strokes. Often the designer wants to simulate wood without indicating any particular variety. The colors used in such a case depend on the effect desired for the set, but a typical example would call for a flat coat of medium brown (Burnt Umber and Whiting) followed by two graining coats, one of Venetian Red and one of Yellow Ocher.

In graining woodwork, care must be taken to make the directions of the strokes match the natural grain of the wood. In a doorframe, for instance, the grain runs horizontally across the top and vertically down the jambs. These meet diagonally at the corners to give the appearance of mitering. Sometimes, as in the case of a paneled door, the directions of the graining are very complicated, and a real door must be examined to learn exactly what pattern to follow.

If our wood is supposed to represent rough boards or is V-grooved ("B" p. 15) it is necessary to draw the cracks. Each crack is made of three lines, a line of dark paint (usually Burnt Umber and Ultramarine mixed) with a line of light wood-color on each side of it to make the crack-line more prominent by contrast.

If the cracks are to be straight they must be lined ("D" p. 111). This is done with a yardstick and the type of brush called an angular liner. The stick is held close to the door and with one end resting against it. The line is then ruled by running the brush along the stick in much the same way that a line is ruled on paper with a pen. The stroke must be made rapidly; otherwise it is likely to wiggle. Care must be taken to keep away from the canvas any part of the yardstick that the brush may touch. If stick, brush, and canvas come together the paint will run under the stick and make a blot.

If the scenery is not to be handled, cracks can be lined with charcoal and highlighted with chalk. Wood should be grained before it is lined.

Snap-lining. So far we have been considering the simpler sorts of scene painting where the only outlines were those furnished by the scene-units themselves. Occasionally, however, the scene painter wants something more elaborate. In old-fashioned melodramas, for instance, the entire set is usually painted on the backdrop. Most non-theatrical artists are accustomed to painting on a fairly small scale and the problem of enlarging a sketch to fit a canvas that may contain several hundred square feet often confuses them. To avoid this difficulty, the sketch is marked off in squares each representing one foot of the finished work. Then the drop is marked with corresponding squares (p. 121). Once this is done it becomes a simple matter to transfer the outline to the drop since each square can be treated as a separate unit.

Ruling the squares on the drop by hand would be a tedious task. Fortunately, a quicker method is available. A piece of stout cotton cord as long as the width of the drop is rubbed with chalk. (Stick chalk will do, but mason's chalk is easier to handle.) Two workers then take the ends of the cord, pull it taut and hold it against the canvas. One worker pulls the cord away from the drop with his free hand and lets it fly back. When the cord is taken away a perfectly straight line of chalk will be left on the canvas. This process is repeated for the remaining lines. It is called **snap-lining** and the cord is called a **snap-line.**

Another method of transferring designs to canvas calls for the use of an **opaque projector.** These projectors are sold in various types and under several trade names, but essentially they are magic lanterns equipped to throw on a screen the images of opaque objects such as drawings, postcards, etc. When used as a scene painting aid, the device is adjusted to project the designer's sketch on the drop, after which it is a simple matter to mark in the outlines with copying pencil or charcoal. The machine requires a darkened room if it is to give good results. It is used only to locate the outlines of the scene, the actual painting being done under ordinary light. Opaque projectors are too expensive to be bought especially for scene painting, but they are available to many amateurs as they are commonly used in schools for visual education.

Wallpaper. Many amateurs use real wallpaper. This works fairly well for one-set plays, though it is a little difficult to get off. If more than one set is involved, paper will not work at all, since it wrinkles when the flats are folded.

Wallpaper patterns can be painted on the canvas. This makes a tedious job but the results frequently justify the trouble. Most wallpaper patterns are of two types: those containing lines or stripes, and those containing irregular patterns such as floral and tree forms. The stripes are first marked out with a snap-line. Then a line is ruled on each side of each stripe with an angular liner and the stripes are filled in with a detail brush.

Irregular patterns are cut from stencil paper and tacked to a frame (p. 121). One worker holds the stencil in place and the other puts on the pattern with a spray gun, which may be borrowed or rented for the purpose. A Flit gun will do, but using it is a slow process. Stencils can also be spattered by hand, but the paint usually runs and the worker holding the stencil gets covered with paint. Stencil paper is 20″ x 24″, so the stenciling process has to be repeated many times before the whole wall is covered. As each design must be placed with great accuracy to obtain the mechanical effect of real wallpaper, guide lines are necessary.

At this stage the pattern is far too strong and must be spattered over with the final spatter coat. This work has to be done carefully. If the spatter is too light the design will be obtrusive, while if the spatter is too heavy the pattern will disappear entirely. An added difficulty springs from the fact that the de-

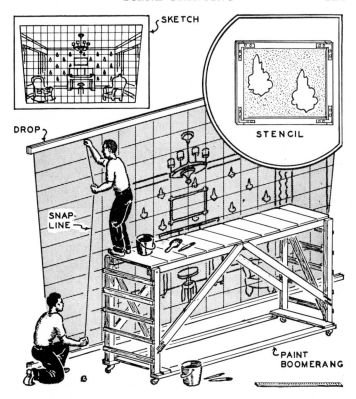

sign shows up more through the wet spatter than it does after the spatter is dry.

Stone. The first scene painting I ever did involved a stone wall. I was proud of it until I learned that it is almost impossible to fail at stone painting. For the best work, the base coat is done with three or four colors, usually dull tones of brown, blue and green. These are applied in irregular patches covering two or three square feet each, and are blended on the canvas while the paint is still wet. This gives a pleasingly irregular effect to the finished work and makes the stone appear weathered. The mortar lines are then painted in with white or light gray ("A" p. 33). Much depends on the way this is done. Amateur painters frequently give themselves away by putting mortar lines on a convex corner, a thing which is impossible in real stone work. The best plan is to copy an actual mortar pattern. When the mortar lines are dry, the whole wall is spattered with a purplish brown made of Ultramarine and Burnt Umber. This gives texture and also tones down the mortar lines which are likely to be overprominent. Finally, each stone should be shadowed with dark paint or charcoal. If further irregularity is desired, cracks and other features can be painted in with a brush.

Brick. Stage bricks may be made in several ways. The easiest is to paint the wall red and then line in the mortar with white. If this looks artificial, a thin spatter of dark blue will give the appearance of texture, or the whole wall may be textured by shadowing each brick with blue or brownish purple. Another method of representing bricks is to paint the flat the color of the mortar, and then paint each individual brick with two strokes of a foliage brush ("F" p. 111). This is not as slow work as it sounds and gives a beautiful effect of irregular brickwork. Horizontal chalk lines should be snapped onto the flat before painting; otherwise it is impossible to keep the courses even. Bricks of this type should be both shadowed and spattered, since they require a depth of texture. Typical shadows are shown on the upper rows of bricks in the sketch. The bricks in the frontispiece were painted by this process. The irregular profile at the edge of the doorway was produced by nailing a piece of $\frac{3}{4}'' \times \frac{3}{4}''$ in the corner and notching out the mortar with a wood rasp. This last trick is responsible for the highly realistic effect obtained.

Leaves are painted with a foliage brush. Each leaf is made with a single stroke, as shown at "C" p. 111. These strokes look square and most unleaflike close up, but at a distance they are very effective. Leaves should not be spotted all over a foliage border like green measles, but should be grouped together in boughs. It is well to lay in a background color in a medium tone and then to paint boughs in light and dark greens.

Convertible Sets. Since convertible sets are to be used over and over, it is well to paint them in such a way that their apparent color will change as much as possible under different conditions of lighting. For this purpose a base coat of Yellow Ocher mixed with Whiting is satisfactory. The first spatter can be Venetian Red and the second spatter Ultramarine mixed with Whiting and a little Chrome Green. The top of the set may then be shadowed with a mixture of Burnt Umber and Ultramarine. When the set is finished it should be a sort of tannish gray under artificial lights. It is well to mix small amounts of color at first and experiment on a test section until the right combination of mixtures and spatter thicknesses is arrived at. A set painted in this fashion includes all the principal colors, and will pick up the hue of whatever light is thrown upon it.

Washing Scenery

After scenery has been painted five or six times the paint becomes so thick it cracks and chips off. When this happens, the scenery must be washed before it can be successfully painted again. Scrubbing brushes and a hose supplied with running water are used for this purpose. The scenery is divided into single units and carried outside to some place where there is air and sunlight but not too much wind. Each scene-unit is stood with its face to a wall so that water from the hose can be sprayed on the back of the canvas until it is thoroughly wet. This dissolves the size that binds the paint to the canvas. The unit is then turned face out and scrubbed with a scrubbing brush. The hose, adjusted to throw a high-pressure stream, is very helpful here both to keep the paint wet and to sluice it off by hydraulic pressure. It is not necessary to wash the canvas clean of stains, but it should be free of all solid paint so that the weave is not clogged.

CHAPTER IX

ASSEMBLING SCENERY

After our scene has been built and painted we are ready to set it up. The first step is to draw a skeleton floor plan, full scale, on the stage floor in chalk. This will enable us to locate each set-unit accurately and will avoid trouble later. The center- and tormentor-lines ("B" p. 31) are snapped in with chalk and all measurements are made from them. Once the scene has been set up and checked, the chalk can be gone over with scene paint. This furnishes a semi-permanent guide for the stagehands in placing the various units during a shift. This painting is unnecessary for one-set shows.

Joining Flats

Although there will be a dozen or more flats in each set, it is unlikely that more than three will have been hinged together in any one group. This will leave several places where the flats must be joined and where there is no possibility of covering the cracks with strippers. This is not serious if the flats meet at a corner, because one flat can overlap the other and keep the audience from seeing through the crack. The overlapping flat should be the one most nearly parallel to the footlights, or, what amounts to the same thing, to the floor boards. This is shown on p. 127 where flat No. 61 overlaps No. 28, and No. 21 overlaps No. 5.

If the flats meet to form a single wall, the crack must either be hidden by some vertical object such as a bell pull, or one flat must be provided with a lip similar to those used in connection with the plug on p. 81. Neither of these devices is really satisfactory and most sets are designed so that the groups of flats come together at a corner. This is the reason for the use of the two small flats marked "8" and "9" in the set at "B" p. 31.

When two flats are brought together so that their faces form an angle of 270°, new difficulties arise, as shown in the inset "B" on p. 127. Note that the edge of flat No. 28 covers ¾" of the back of No. 61 so that if the profile-blocks had not been held back, they would have prevented a neat joint.

Nailing. The simplest way to join two flats that meet at an angle is to nail them together with 8d finishing nails. Four nails are enough. The heads should project slightly so that they can easily be withdrawn when the set is dismantled.

Lashing. If the scenery is to be shifted, nailing is out of the question, and the flats must be **lashed** together with ¼" sash cord which zigzags down the rear of the joint and is caught on metal projections, called **lash-cleats,** attached to the stiles (p. 127). In the discussion which follows, "right" and "left" refer to the point of view of a person standing behind the flats.

The **lash-line** is attached to the upper right-hand corner of the left flat through a hole in the corner-block ("A"). A knot is tied on the far end of the line and the line is pulled back until the knot jams against the inside of the block. The top lash-cleat is screwed to the inner edge of the left stile of the right-hand flat 1′ 0″ from the top. The next cleat is placed 3′ 0″ lower on the left-hand flat and followed by a third cleat 3′ 0″ farther down on the right-hand flat. If the normal spacing of the cleats brings them within 3″ of a corner-brace or toggle-bar, they must be placed slightly higher or lower; otherwise it will be difficult to slip the lash-line around them. Note that if the corner-braces were placed on the left of the flat, the top brace would interfere to some extent with the process of getting the line over the top cleat. For this reason it is standard practice to place the braces on the right as shown in the illustrations.

When cleats are not available, No. 12 screws or even 12d common nails may be substituted. This is an unfortunate practice, as the strain of the lashing on such makeshifts may split the stile and ruin the whole flat.

When the flats meet at an angle of 270° as do No. 61 and No. 28 in the drawing, the lashing instead of holding their edges together, tends to pull them apart. Thus No. 28 would be pulled to the left. This can be prevented by the use of **stop-blocks** ("B"), three of which are used at each such joint. The blocks are 6″ long and made of 1″ x 2″. Two $\frac{7}{32}$″ holes are bored to take the $1\frac{1}{2}$″ x 9 screws that hold them to the back of the overlapping flat (No. 61). Stop-blocks must also be used on the tormentors (p. 7).

The bottom end of the lash-line is tied off around two **lash-hooks** ("D" p. 127). These are screwed to the inside edge of the stiles 2′ 6″ from the floor and are placed with their hooked ends up. Note that the line is not tied in a knot but is merely caught under the hooks and looped behind its own upper part. The hooks permit the lashing to be drawn very tight and also make it possible to tie or loosen the line in an instant.

Lash-cleats may be substituted for hooks in an emergency, but they are not recommended since it is difficult to tie the line around them without leaving some slack. Many different tie-off knots have been devised for use with lash-cleats. The one shown at "E" is perhaps the best. "F" in the large drawing shows the first step in making this knot.

Occasionally door flats such as No. 2 on p. 10 are built with the inner stiles so close to the outer stiles that there is no room for lash-cleats. When this is the case, lash-hooks placed horizontally with their hooked ends toward the edge of the flat, and 3″ from it, are used instead of cleats.

To lash flats, we bring them together in the proper position and flick a line over the top cleat on the right-hand flat. This is done by grasping the line near the bottom, and giving it a quick snap with the wrist. Lashing takes some practice, but once the knack is acquired, it is easy. The secret lies in two things. First: make the throw as high as possible; many failures result from too low a throw, but it is difficult to overshoot the cleat too far. Second: when the line is thrown it must be pulled back with a jerk; the line is in position to catch the cleat for only a moment, so too slow a jerk will miss entirely.

The line is snapped over the top cleat on the left-hand flat

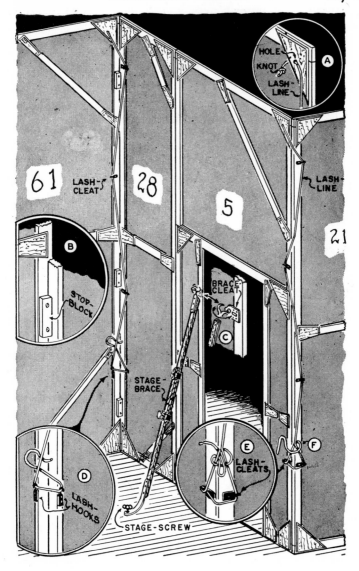

in the same way. The other cleats can usually be handled by holding the line taut with the right hand and slipping it over the cleat with the left.

Bracing

Two flats joined at right angles will stand alone, but in all other positions they must be braced. Braces must also be placed on each side of the opening in a door flat.

An elementary form of brace is shown in "A" p. 15. It consists of a piece of $1'' \times 3''$ with its ends cut at an angle. A block of $2'' \times 4''$ is nailed to the floor, and the brace is nailed to it and to an upright of the scene-unit.

Stage-braces (p. 127) are the most useful type of brace. They are adjustable and can be placed or removed quickly and without noise. They may also be put to a number of secondary uses, such as hooking a lash-line over a high cleat in a tight corner.

It is cheaper to make braces than to buy them. The necessary hardware consists of a **hook,** a **heel** and a set of **clamps.** The shafts should be of maple or other hard wood. They must be exactly $1\frac{5}{16}'' \times 1\frac{1}{8}''$ and have their edges rounded or beveled. It is well to have two sizes of braces. The shorter size uses two $4'\,0''$ lengths of wood and may be adjusted for lengths from $5'\,0''$ to $8'\,4''$. The longer size uses $5'\,0''$ lengths and will extend from $6'\,0''$ to $10'\,4''$. Three or four short braces and five or six long ones will handle almost any production.

The brace is attached to the flat by means of a **brace-cleat** ("C"). This is a flat piece of metal which is screwed to a stile, and has a hole in the free end in which the hook of the brace may be caught. To place a brace in a cleat, the brace is turned so that its heel points to the floor. One of the horns of the hook is now passed through the eye of the cleat from back to front (counting the side toward the canvas as the front). The brace is then turned over so that the free horn rests in a rectangular slot in the cleat. This turn brings the bottom of the heel parallel with the floor, to which it is fastened by placing a **stage-screw** in one of the holes provided for the purpose.

Stage-screws are shaped like thumbscrews but are so large that the top can be grasped by the hand and the screw twisted into the ordinary stage floor. If the floor is of hard wood, a small hole may have to be bored first. Such a hole can be marked with a dab of white paint so that it can be easily found during the scene shift. The best quality stage-screws are worth their additional cost. Cheap ones do not last long and make bigger holes. Even the finest screws soon become blunt and must be sharpened with a triangular file. A dull stage-screw is a curse. Keep yours sharp. Stage-screws go in more easily if placed in a crack of the floor.

Large screw eyes can be substituted for stage-screws in an emergency.

Groups that are cursed with hardwood floors too sacred for stage-screws will find a solution in the **stage weight** ("E" p. 69) designed by Arthur C. Cloetingh, Director of Dramatics at Pennsylvania State College. This is merely a 50-pound lead weight 12″ x 6″ x 4″ with felt glued to the bottom and handles of $\frac{3}{8}$″ iron rod let into each end. A hole is started in the top with a 30d nail and the stage-screw placed in the hole. If the hole becomes too loose it can be closed up with a few well-directed hammer blows.

The Clancy Company also makes a device for this purpose. It is called a **non-skid floor-plate** and costs $1.50. Unfortunately it requires a 25-pound weight as an accessory and so has little if any advantage over the home-made article.

Brace-jacks ("F" p. 99) are sometimes substituted for stage-braces. They are made of 1″ x 3″ and held together with bolts and mending-plates. Flat footirons are screwed to the bottom members and held to the floor with stage-screws. Since they must be folded out of the way when not in use, the jacks are attached to the scene-unit with pin-hinges. Jacks are to be preferred to stage-braces in some ways, as they not only steady the top of the scene-unit but hold its lower edge in place as well. On the other hand, they make the scene shift somewhat awkward and this, plus the fact that they cannot be adjusted, accounts for the fact that they are rarely used.

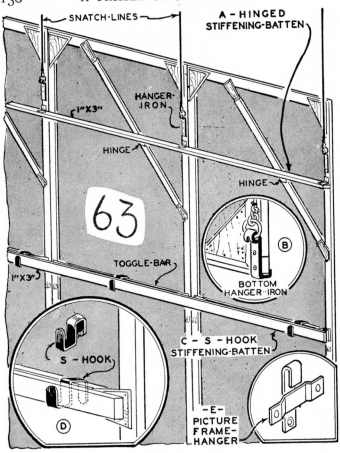

SNATCH-LINES

A – HINGED STIFFENING-BATTEN

HANGER-IRON

1"X3"

HINGE

HINGE

63

BOTTOM HANGER-IRON B

TOGGLE-BAR

1"X3"

C – S-HOOK STIFFENING-BATTEN

S – HOOK

D

–E– PICTURE FRAME-HANGER

Stiffening

As the walls of a set are only ¾" thick and are hinged at intervals of 5′ 9″ or less, they will bend in the center unless stiffened in some way. Braces must provide some of this stiffening and for ordinary purposes the weight of the ceiling will supply the rest. Often, however, greater rigidity is needed and must be furnished by **stiffening-battens.**

"C" p. 130 shows the simplest type of stiffening-batten, a length of 1″ x 3″ attached to the toggle-bars with **S-hooks.** This explains why all toggle-bars are placed at the same height. If they varied by even a few inches, they could not be used to hold a stiffener. Where openings in the wall make it impossible to place the stiffener on the toggle-bars, it can be hung behind the upper rails on S-hooks slipped over the top of the flat.

Where a wall is to be shifted as a unit, another method of stiffening is employed. This is shown at "A." Note that the batten, made of 1″ x 3″, is placed edgewise to the flats so that its greatest depth comes in the direction of the strain. The batten is attached to the flats with tight-pin backflaps, or, if the wall must be folded at any time, with pin-hinges. Note how the hinges are placed alternately above and below the batten. These hinges, like those used on tree trunks, do not fold but are merely a convenient device for joining two pieces of wood. It is well to use two such stiffening-battens, one near the top of the walls and one near the bottom. The lower batten must be made in several parts if there are doorways in the wall. Walls over 16′ 0″ cannot be taken care of by a single upper batten, so two overlapping 1″ x 3″s must be used.

Placing Other Scene-Units

Scene-units other than flats are kept in place by a variety of devices.

Footirons. Most scene-units depend on their weight to hold them in position on the stage floor. If a stronger attachment is needed, it can be supplied by corner-irons and ⅞″ x 9 screws, or, if a shift is necessary, by footirons and stage-screws.

Footirons are of three types. The common, or solid, foot-iron is shown at "D" p. 145. The upright part is screwed to the scene-unit and the horizontal part is fastened to the floor with a stage-screw. Hinged footirons are similar except that they permit the scene-unit to meet the floor at any angle and may be folded when not in use. They are so rarely needed that I cannot recall having seen one. Flat footirons have already been mentioned (p. 129 and "F" p. 99). They are occasionally attached to the bottom of tree trunks that are unsteady and might fall over unless fastened to the floor.

Hinges. Scene-units, such as a doorframe and its flat, that must be held rigidly together and yet will have to be separated for the scene shift, are frequently joined by strap hinges or pin-hinges. When used in this way, they rarely function as hinges, but are merely convenient joining devices like lash-lines or turnbuttons.

"C" p. 87 shows how the frame of a door, window, or bookcase is clamped to its flat with strap hinges. One such hinge is attached to each side of the frame, 5′ 0″ from the floor. The hinges are screwed on at a slight angle with their lower ends forward. The bottom of the frame is first placed in the opening. Then the free leaves of the hinges are knocked up and the frame is tilted into place. When the leaves of the hinges are pulled down, they wedge against the inner stiles of the flat and lock the frame firmly in position.

In modernistic sets where the frames have no facings but are merely thickness-pieces, another method must be used. Such frames fit on the back of the flat, flush with the edges of the opening. This means that the profile-blocks must be held back and usually that the opening must be plugged to make it the exact size of the frame. If no shift is required, the frame can be attached to the flat with corner-irons, but if a shift is necessary, pin-hinges are used instead. The frame is held in place temporarily with small nails, and two pin-hinges are then screwed to the outside of each jamb and to the backs of the inner stiles of the flat. When the nails and pins are removed, the frame may easily be separated from the flat. It can be put back in place and held by simply replacing the pins.

A good many joints are made with pin-hinges, but the method is not altogether satisfactory as it is often difficult to replace the pins. This can be partially overcome by substituting 8d finishing nails bent in the same L-shape as the pins. The nails go in better than the original pins, as they are pointed and somewhat smaller.

Hooks. Light pieces are often kept in place with **picture frame-hangers** ("E" p. 130), which are like hooks-and-eyes made of flat metal. The socket is screwed to one of the units to be joined, and the hook to the other. This is more difficult than it seems because two pairs of hangers are usually required and it is not easy to locate them so that they match exactly. These hangers are used not only for picture frames but for other light objects as well. Thus, if the scene at "C" p. 31 must be shifted, the railing on stage right may be attached to the doorframe with one of them.

Pictures can be hung in another way that the amateur will often find more satisfactory. An S-hook is slipped over the top of the flat, with its free side to the front, and the picture supported from this by a cord. Both cord and hook should be colored to match the flat. If the set must be shifted it is well to tie a loop at the top of the cord so that when the loop is in place on the hook, the picture will automatically hang straight.

A third sort of hook is the wire kind usually associated with screen doors. These have no set use, but they will serve in many miscellaneous cases where strength is not required. It is well to try them when circumstances permit, as they are the most rapid of all joining devices.

Hanging Scenery. Certain types of scenery including ceilings, drops, borders, and drapery units, must be hung from above. Drapes are occasionally suspended from 2″ x 4″ wooden battens supported by uprights, standing on the stage floor, and a similar system, involving a framework of pipe, is sometimes used for cycloramas. For the most part, however, the support is furnished by ropes that are either attached directly to the gridiron or run over pulleys. The latter system is better and will be described in detail on p. 137.

The lines holding a ceiling are tied to rings bolted to the long members (p. 141). Lines carrying drops and borders may be attached to screw eyes in the batten, but a safer method is to tie them around the batten itself through holes cut in the canvas directly below the wood.

Cycloramas, supported from overhead, demand pipe-battens and arms, also of pipe, which are attached to the main batten by special cyclorama knuckles. The individual drapes are tied to the batten by 1' 6" lengths of stout cord run through the grommets in the upper hem.

CHAPTER X

SCENE SHIFTING

The methods used to change scenes have been less completely worked out than those employed in the other departments of stagecraft. One reason for this is that each play and each stage presents a special problem, so that stock solutions are impossible.

Scenery is shifted in two directions. We **set** a piece of scenery by bringing it from the wings and putting it in its proper place on stage. The opposite process, taking a piece from the stage and storing it in the wings, is called **striking.** These terms apply whether the object set or struck is an ash tray, a flat, or a whole set. Amateur stages are rarely large enough to permit complete sets to be changed as units, so each scene must be broken up into parts which are shifted separately. The methods of handling these parts are described below. The reader will have to make his own decisions as to which methods to use in any particular case.

Running

When scenery is shifted by hand with no mechanical assistance, the process is called **running.** Walls are folded and slid along the floor; other objects are picked up bodily and carried. Running is laborious and slow, but it involves no technical problems and for this reason is recommended to the novice.

Handling flats requires some practice. Though not heavy, they are large and unwieldy, and if they are leaned too far over, the leverage conferred by their height becomes formidable. The first rule in running a flat, therefore, is to keep it erect. One man can handle a flat, but with beginners it is safer to use two. To avoid air resistance, the flat is moved edgewise. The man in front lifts his edge a little from the floor. It is his business to guide as well as to supply most of the power. The man in back pushes, but his main purpose is to balance the flat and keep it from toppling over; he should not lift. The rear end of the lower rail must remain in contact with the floor; otherwise the flat will pivot between the hands of the workers.

If several flats are hinged together, they may be folded and handled as a single flat.

A flat can be laid on the floor by simply putting a foot against the bottom rail and letting go. The air resistance acts as a brake and the flat will settle as gracefully as a bird. This trick is called **floating.** It can be worked with a group of hinged flats, if they are unfolded to gain the maximum air resistance. It should not be attempted with a single flat that has an opening built in it, as the opening adds to the weight and cuts down the air resistance.

Lowering a hinged group of flats to the floor without unfolding requires three men. Two of them stand on one side of the flat grasping the stiles. The third stands on the other side and places his foot against the lower rail. The other two walk away from him, working up the stiles with a hand-over-hand movement until they reach the top rail, when they can lower the flats to the floor without difficulty. This method is known as **walking down.** To **walk up** a group of flats, the process is reversed.

Handling Doors. Doors and doorframes are shifted as a unit, but they should never be handled as part of a flat. One of the first steps in striking a set is to take the frames from the walls and stand them in the center of the stage out of the way until the walls can be struck. If the doors are opened, the frames will stand by themselves. A frame is never dragged along the ground, but must be picked up and carried by two men who should tilt it at an angle so that the door stays closed of its own weight.

Flying

In even moderately well-equipped theaters, all hung scenery is supported by lines which run over pulleys attached to the gridiron and are controlled from the pin rail. This system makes it possible to raise the scene-units (and overhead lighting equipment as well) from the floor. If the gridiron is high, there may be enough fly space to permit ceilings, drops, borders, back walls, and even whole sets to be flown in this manner and stored out of the way overhead.

Rigging. The rigging which was described briefly on p. 7 may now be explained in detail. One or more sets of lines are needed for each unit to be flown. These lines are sometimes attached directly to the scenery, but a better plan is to tie them to battens of $1\frac{1}{4}''$ pipe which should be somewhat longer than the proscenium is wide. The offstage ends of the lines are tied around the pins of the pin rail.

Scene-units are hung from the pipe-battens with lengths of $\frac{1}{4}''$ or $\frac{3}{8}''$ rope called **snatch-lines.**

Knots. The **bowline** (p. 139), the **fisherman's bend** (p. 139), and the knot called **two half-hitches** ("A" p. 99) are the principal knots used in rigging. The knots used to tie off lash-lines are shown on p. 127, and the one used to tie off main lines to a pin rail is illustrated on p. 139. In many knots it is well to fasten the end of the rope to its main part with friction tape. This will avoid any possibility of having the knot come untied.

Sandbags. Amateur scenery is rarely heavy enough to require counterweighting. When necessary, it is usually provided in the form of sandbags attached to the offstage ends of the rigging lines. Strong, professionally made bags are needed. A weak bag may split, lose its load of sand, and drop the flown scenery on the head of anyone standing below. I have had no personal experience with sandbags, but the method of using them is simple enough. The scene-unit is pulled up by hand until it hangs close to the gridiron. A **clamp** is then fastened to the offstage side of the lines at a point just higher than a man's head and the bag is attached to the bottom of the clamp. The weight of the bag should be at least twenty or thirty pounds lighter than that of the flown scenery as there is no way to pull the scenery down and its own weight must take care of this. Rope stretches and contracts with the amount of humidity in the air and the variation is greater in the long line than in the short line. For this reason it may be necessary to trim the lines every day by readjusting the clamp.

If pipe-battens are not available, a small sandbag must be attached to the onstage ends of each set of lines when they are not in use. Otherwise it will be difficult to get them down again when needed.

Counterweight System. The rigging system just described is known as the **ropeline system** to distinguish it from the **counterweight system,** diagrammed on p. 139, which uses steel cable. The counterweight system is very elaborate and expensive, and must be installed by a professional rigging company. Unless the reader expects to work on a stage equipped with a counterweight system or is studying this book as part of a course in stagecraft, he may profitably skip this section.

The pulleys in the ropeline system can be moved along the grid beams to any point desired. In the counterweight system no such adjustment is possible, so a set of lines must be installed at every point at which it may be desirable to fly a piece of scenery. This makes it necessary to have from twenty to thirty sets of lines on a stage of medium depth.

Each unit of the system consists of a pipe-batten, a set of three or four main lines made of steel cable, a set of **loft-blocks** (pulleys), a **counterweight carriage,** a **purchase-line,** and a **lock-rail** (which corresponds to the pin rail of a ropeline system). Numerous examples are illustrated in the Clancy catalog.

The counterweight carriage is attached to the offstage ends of the main lines and serves to hold the iron **counterweights** which balance any load of scenery tied to the pipe-batten. The carriages slide in vertical guides (not shown) so that there is no danger of one carriage swinging sideways and **fouling** another.

The purchase-line is made of heavy rope. It is tied to the top of the carriage, passes over a sheave in the head-block, and comes down through a locking clamp in the lock-rail. From there it runs under another sheave called a **floor-block** and

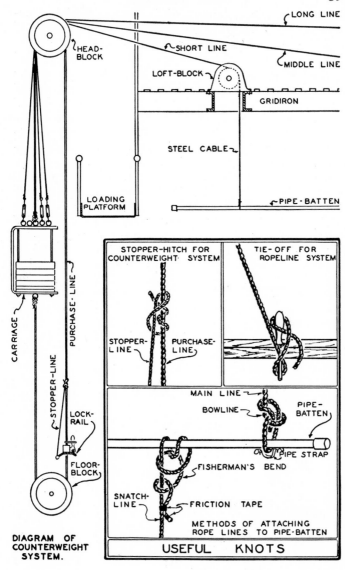

LONG LINE

SHORT LINE

MIDDLE LINE

HEAD-BLOCK

LOFT-BLOCK

GRIDIRON

STEEL CABLE

LOADING PLATFORM

PIPE-BATTEN

CARRIAGE

PURCHASE-LINE

STOPPER-LINE

LOCK-RAIL

FLOOR-BLOCK

DIAGRAM OF COUNTERWEIGHT SYSTEM.

STOPPER-HITCH FOR COUNTERWEIGHT SYSTEM

STOPPER-LINE

PURCHASE-LINE

TIE-OFF FOR ROPELINE SYSTEM

MAIN LINE

BOWLINE

PIPE-BATTEN

FISHERMAN'S BEND

SNATCH-LINE

FRICTION TAPE

PIPE STRAP

METHODS OF ATTACHING ROPE LINES TO PIPE-BATTEN

USEFUL KNOTS

is carried upward until it can be tied to the bottom of the counterweight carriage. A pull downward on the onstage side of the purchase-line lifts the carriage and lowers the pipe-batten. A pull on the offstage side of the line lowers the carriage and lifts the batten. The clamp on the lock-rail binds on the purchase-line and keeps it from moving. The clamp is not very strong and cannot be depended upon, unless the flown scenery is perfectly balanced. When either the scenery is heavier than the counterweight, or *vice versa,* a **stopper-line** must be used. One end of this is attached to the lock-rail and the other end tied around the purchase-line with a **stopper-hitch.**

Another essential part of a counterweight system is the **loading platform.** This is a metal cat-walk running up- and down-stage about fifteen feet below the gridiron and directly in front of the purchase-lines. When a piece of scenery is to be counterweighted, it is first attached to the pipe-batten with snatch-lines. A stagehand standing on the loading platform now places counterweights on the carriage until a balance is reached and the scenery can be easily lifted by one man. If the carriage includes a device for fastening the counterweights in place, this device should be used. If such a device is lacking, the heaviest counterweight must be placed on top as light ones may bounce off and cause serious accidents.

Although a counterweight system is complicated in description, it is so simple in operation that anyone who remembers to place the heaviest weight on top and to tie off unbalanced loads with stopper-lines should have no difficulty in flying any scene element except a back wall. The special problems connected with back walls are discussed on p. 142.

Drops and borders should be hung from pipe-battens with snatch-lines ("A" p. 99). The wooden battens that are part of the unit are rarely stiff enough to make it practical to hang them directly from the main lines of the rigging.

Rigging roll ceilings requires two battens ("B" p. 141) but otherwise they are even more easily rigged than drops, since they already have rings to receive the snatch-lines.

The gridirons on most amateur stages are so low that the ceiling can barely be lifted high enough for the set to be moved

CEILING RIGGINGS

A - BOOK CEILING

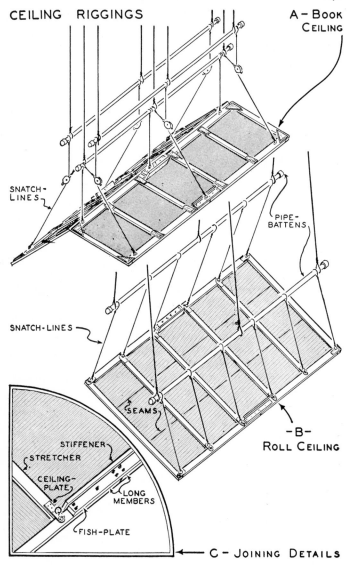

SNATCH-LINES

PIPE-BATTENS

SNATCH-LINES

SEAMS

-B-
ROLL CEILING

STIFFENER

STRETCHER

CEILING-PLATE

LONG MEMBERS

FISH-PLATE

C - JOINING DETAILS

under it. With a grid height of 30′ 0″ or more, however, it is possible to manipulate the battens so that the ceiling hangs vertically in the flies supported only by the back batten. When it is in this position any other flown scenery such as drops, borders, and even the back walls of sets can be raised or lowered without the ceiling's being in the way.

Where the ceiling can be flown in this fashion, it is well to bolt pieces of 1″ x 3″ to the side walls of the sets 2′ 0″ or 3′ 0″ from the tormentor and projecting 6″ or more above the set. These serve as **stops** and keep the ceiling from sliding too far downstage when it is lowered.

Book ceilings demand a more complicated rigging ("A" p. 141). Three pipe-battens are used. The middle one supports the ceiling when flown, and its snatch-lines are tied to rings bolted to the downstage half of the ceiling near the hinge. To this pipe-batten are also attached pulleys by lines a foot or so long. Through these pulleys run snatch-lines from the other pipe-battens to the up- and down-stage edges of the ceiling.

To raise the ceiling all three battens are lifted until the ceiling is clear of the set. Then the middle batten is raised still farther. This automatically slacks off the snatch-lines running to the other two battens and the ceiling folds by its own weight. Finally, all three pipe-battens are raised until the ceiling is lifted completely out of the way.

To lower the ceiling it is first brought down until it is clear of any other scenery that may be hanging in the flies. It is then opened by lowering the middle pipe-batten and at the same time raising the other two. Lastly, all three battens are lowered together until the ceiling rests on top of the set.

There is nothing to be gained by using such a complicated mechanism except on stages where the grid is from 20′ 0″ to 30′ 0″ high. A grid within these limits gives room to fly and store a book ceiling but does not provide the height required to store a roll ceiling. For gridirons less than 20′ 0″ or more than 30′ 0″, a roll ceiling should be preferred.

Flying Back Walls. A back wall that is to be parallel to the curtain line, or nearly so, can be flown if there is height enough in the flies to receive it. The method of doing this is shown on p. 130. The wall is first stiffened with hinged stiffening-battens. **Hanger-irons** are then bolted to the stiles just below the corner-blocks, and snatch-lines are tied to them and to the pipe-batten. Long snatch-lines are needed here as the ceiling, when in place, will project a foot or more in back of the set and the snatch-lines must be slackened enough to permit this.

If the wall is heavy, **bottom hanger-irons** ("B") should be added. These bolt to the bottom ends of the stiles and have hooks which catch under the rail and support the weight of the flat. The snatch-lines are tied to the rings of the bottom hanger-iron and led through (but not tied to) the rings in the top hanger-iron. This keeps the wall upright. If bottom hanger-irons are not necessary, they should not be used, as they must be countersunk in the rail and this damages the flat.

When a back wall is flown with a counterweight system, slacking off the snatch-lines becomes a serious problem because the counterweight is no longer balanced by the scenery and must be supported entirely by the purchase-line. Under these circumstances, the clamp on the lock-rail is much too weak to be effective and two or three stopper-lines must be tied around the purchase-line for safety. Even so, too many risks are involved in the process for the novice to attempt it.

Rolling

The quickest and easiest way of shifting scenery is by mounting it on **casters.**

Scenery arranged for rolling takes up a great deal of storage space, so it must be carefully planned. Otherwise you may be caught in the embarrassing position of completing your sets only to find that they cannot be shifted. I speak from experience. This almost happened to me on one occasion and I was saved only by a lucky fluke. Such a situation can be avoided by working out the shift on a measured drawing of the stage with cardboard models, made to scale, of each item involved.

Rollers on Platforms. Ordinary platforms can be mounted

on casters with ease. A 2″ x 4″ is placed between each pair of legs and held in place by two corner-irons at each end ("D" p. 145). The casters are screwed to the bottom of the 2″ x 4″. A platform equipped in this way moves at a touch and must be fastened to the floor with footirons and stage-screws; otherwise an actor may step on it and go sailing off into the wings at the most inopportune moment.

Very low platforms are made as shown at "A." These are called **wagons** and are often so large that a whole set can be mounted on them. Small wagons are also very useful, and will probably appeal to the amateur, as ordinary platform tops can be easily converted for this purpose. The bottom boards are of 1″ x 6″ yellow pine. They work on the same principle as the lower member of a truss and make the platform rigid while adding only ¾″ to its thickness. The rollers are screwed to 1′ 6″ pieces of 2″ x 4″ which, in turn, are bolted to the floor boards with 2½″ stove bolts. Note that the boards immediately above the rollers bear the whole weight of the platform, which, in fact, actually hangs from these boards. To make this possible, the boards are held to the 2″ x 4″ with 5″ carriage bolts as shown in "b" sketch "A."

Larger platforms may be built on the same model. The 2″ x 4″s should not be much over 2′ 0″ apart, nor should the casters be separated by more than 8′ 0″. A 14′ 0″ x 16′ 0″ wagon would thus call for nine casters arranged in three rows of three.

Any rolling unit must clear the floor by at least ½″, and ¾″ is better. Otherwise it may sag a little and drag on the floor.

Rolling Jacks. A large wall can be handled as a unit by means of **tip-jacks.** These are somewhat like ordinary brace-jacks in appearance ("B" p. 145). The bottom rail makes an angle of 75° with the main upright. The inset shows how pieces of 1″ x 4″ are placed under the jacks and attached with 2″ x 2″ blocks. This 1″ x 4″ must withstand a great strain, as the casters are screwed to the bottom.

The wall is stiffened with hinged stiffening-battens to which the jacks are attached by corner-irons and diagonal braces. When in use the wall is held upright by ordinary stage-braces.

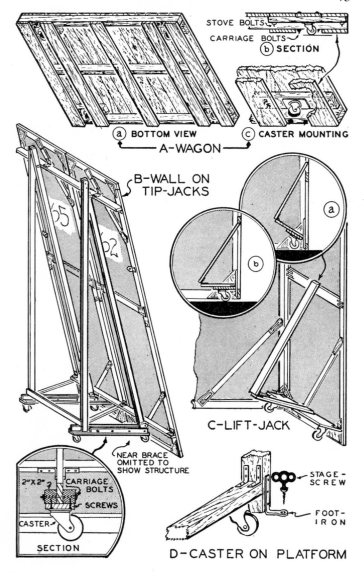

STOVE BOLTS

CARRIAGE BOLTS

(b) SECTION

(a) BOTTOM VIEW   (c) CASTER MOUNTING

A-WAGON

B-WALL ON TIP-JACKS

(a)

(b)

C-LIFT-JACK

NEAR BRACE OMITTED TO SHOW STRUCTURE

2"X 2"   CARRIAGE BOLTS

SCREWS

CASTER

SECTION

STAGE-SCREW

FOOT-IRON

D-CASTER ON PLATFORM

To strike the set, these braces are removed, after which the wall is tipped back upon the casters for rolling. Walls over 20′ 0″ wide will require three tip-jacks.

Another rolling device is called a **lift-jack.** One type * is shown at "C." This is hinged to the piece of scenery. The scenery rests on the floor when the jack is raised, as shown in the main drawing and in the inset marked "a." To lift the scenery onto the casters a stagehand steps on the end of the jack. This lowers the hinged arm which can now be caught under the toggle-bar as shown in "b." Notice that the scenery now clears the floor by an inch or more.

A simpler form of this device consists of a piece of 1″ x 6″ hinged at one end with a single caster placed under it. When in use the free end of this type of lift-jack is held down by a bent brace-cleat which is fastened at a convenient point on the scenery. A screw driven part way into the 1″ x 6″ catches in the hole of the brace-cleat and keeps the jack from slipping loose.

Lift-jacks are chiefly used in connection with alcoves, large chimney-breasts, and other light three-dimensional forms. In most cases two or more such jacks must be employed on each scene-element that is to be rolled in this manner.

Routining a Shift

Although a well-devised shifting method is important, proper drilling of the stagehands is even more so. A rapid shift requires that no one should be idle, and no one should be given a task that he cannot carry out quickly. This takes careful planning and a number of rehearsals as well; otherwise all sorts of awkward situations may arise. Badly drilled crews will frequently set a whole scene only to discover that a large table has not been placed and that a wall has to be torn out before the table can be brought on stage.

Most pieces of scenery can be handled by two stagehands, so it is well to plan the work in pairs. The number of pairs needed depends on the method used in shifting and the amount

* *Scenery for the Theatre,* Burris-Meyer & Cole.

	1ST PAIR	2ND PAIR	3RD PAIR	4TH PAIR
	TOM and BILL	SAM and PETE	ED and DICK	DAN and LUKE
STEP I	Strike A 6	Move door in A 2	Move door in A 3	Raise ceiling
STEP II	Strike A 7 including window	Strike A 1	Strike A 3	Strike A 4
STEP III	Strike A 5	Strike A 2 Strike center chair	Strike A 3 door	Strike stage left chairs
STEP IV	Strike stage right chairs	Strike A 2 door	Strike table	Strike desk
STEP V	Move B 3 door	Set B 3	Set B 5	Set B 4
STEP VI	Set B 3 door	Set B 6	Set B 8	Set B 2
STEP VII	Set B 1	Set railings	Set B 7	Lower ceiling

SHIFT CHART

of scenery to be handled. For the average play, eight boys will be enough. Too many stagehands are as bad as too few, as they will get in each other's way, and the extra ones are likely to feel that they are not needed and will take little interest in the work.

Before attempting to rehearse the stagehands, it is well to work out the shifts with **plan models** of the sets. In these models each scene-unit is represented by a piece of cardboard cut to the shape the unit would have on the floor plan ("B" p. 31 and "C" p. 39). If several scene-units are shifted as one, the same piece of cardboard will serve for all of them. The flats can be thin strips of cardboard of lengths corresponding to the scale widths of the flats they represent. (A strip $2\frac{1}{4}''$ long would stand for a $4'$ $6''$ flat, if the model is made to a scale of $\frac{1}{2}'' = 1'$ $0''$, as is usual.) These strips can be joined together with hinges made of threads held in place with drops of glue. Each article of furniture should also be represented by a piece of cardboard. It usually takes more time to shift the furniture than it does the scenery. When a complete model of this type has been made for each set, the shifts can be gone through experimentally. This should be done on a plan of the stage so that the exact amount of stacking space at any point can be taken into account.

A shift is too complicated to be thought of as a whole, so it is divided into steps. Each step should be so arranged that it will have the same amount of work for each pair of stagehands. One pair, for instance, should not be expected to set a heavy wall while another moves a small table.

As the routine is planned it must be recorded on a chart like that on p. 147, which shows how the set at "A" p. 31 could be changed to the set at "C." (For this purpose the scenes should be thought of as separate sets and not as different arrangements of the same convertible set.) To save space on the chart, the verb "set" is used only when an object is to be placed in its final position on stage. Similarly "strike" means that the object is to be placed in its final storage position. When an object is to be placed in some temporary position, the word "move" is used. For example, the doors are first "moved" onstage to get them out of the walls (Step I), then they are "struck" (Steps III and IV). In ordinary stage parlance this whole process would be called "striking the doors."

Each step should prepare for the next. Thus the ceiling must be raised before the walls can be struck. The shift shown in the chart does not provide any complicated example of this requirement, but sometimes they are very involved and a whole series of steps must be performed in a certain sequence if the shift is to flow smoothly.

Each stagehand should be given a copy of his duties typed on a $3''$ x $5''$ card. When changes are made, the cards should be collected and re-typed. These cards are a great help and should be handed out before the first shift rehearsal. An example of one of them is shown below.

In rehearsals, each step should be carried out separately. When the curtain comes down, the stage manager shouts "Strike," which is the signal for the first step. The leader of each pair should call his number as the pair finishes its task. This makes it easy to tell if the work has been fairly apportioned. If a mistake is made or a difficulty encountered, the stage manager or the head stagehand (called the **stage carpenter**) should blow a whistle for all work to stop until the

```
    TOM (with Bill)        ACT I to ACT II

   I: -  Strike A  6

  II: -  Strike A  7  (including window)

 III: -  Strike A  5

  IV: -  Strike stage right chairs

   V: -  Move B  3 door

  VI: -  Set B  3  door

 VII: -  Set  B  1
```

STAGEHAND'S SHIFT CARD

trouble is corrected. When the first step has been completed correctly the second step is called, and so on. If this method is followed in rehearsal, each stagehand should understand his duties and be able to perform them smoothly and swiftly.

A stage crew is a team in which each member plays a definite part. Each must attend all technical and dress rehearsals, and all performances. An actor who misses a performance ruins the play. A stagehand who misses a performance may ruin it in a more subtle manner by breaking up the team work of the crew. This may add five minutes or more to each shift.

Boring an audience for even one minute after the curtain should have gone up is a cardinal sin in the theater.

On the other hand, if a crew does function as a team, no part of stagecraft is as much fun as scene shifting. It is a sort of team golf, where the object is to reduce the number of movements and thus save time. Every rehearsal shift should be timed, as it adds greatly to the crew's interest if it is able to "keep score."

On the evenings of performances, all stagehands should wear soft-soled shoes. They must reach the theater in plenty of time to have the stage set half an hour before the curtain is to open, so that the electrician can have an opportunity to focus his lights. Stagehands should not stand in the wings while the play is going on, if there is a green room or other place where they can wait. It is the duty of the stage manager to call them shortly before the end of each scene. They then tip-toe to their proper positions and stand ready for the cry of "Strike!" This is given just as in rehearsal and is not audible to the audience, which is (presumably) applauding. The actual change should be made smoothly and not in separated steps as in rehearsal. As each stagehand finishes his duties, he should move out of sight-lines. When all are finished, the stage carpenter reports to the stage manager that the scene is set. When everything is ready the stage manager says "Clear stage!", which means that everyone who is in sight-lines (except the actors for that scene) should run for the wings so that the curtain may be opened.

CHAPTER XI

CONCLUSION

We have now covered the principal methods employed in stagecraft, or at least in that part of it which has to do with the design, construction, painting, and handling of scenery. If the reader finds some of these methods too complicated, I can answer only that the trouble lies more in the difficulty of explaining a mechanical situation in print than in any complication in the processes themselves.

Those who are in search of simplicity can gain it at will. For their benefit, it may be well to restate here, in the form of rules, the various ways of reducing the cost and effort of scene building:

1. Select a play that needs only one set (preferably an interior, to avoid sight-line problems), and that does not involve elaborate or unusual features.
2. Design scenery that can be assembled from stock units, and that requires few or no specials.
3. Avoid unnecessary work-consuming features such as curved walls, arches, applied ornaments, etc.
4. Choose simple paint patterns, preferably those that call for nothing but flat coat and spatter or dry brushing.
5. If you are restricted to a cyclorama set or a convertible set, do not choose a play without making sure that the set can be arranged to meet the requirements of that play.

You will not want to follow these rules. No one does. It is far more fun to do elaborate spectacles and devise interesting scene shifts, but that is up to you. Scenery can be as complicated or as simple as you care to make it.

In any event, do not overlook the more difficult branches of the subject because you believe them to be beyond your present means or skill. The more we know about the stage, the more we are able to use a simplicity that may be forced upon us.

CURTAIN

INDEX

Definitions of a few terms not covered by the main text are included. References printed in boldface type indicate illustrations.

Abe Lincoln in Illinois, 36.

Anna Christie, 17.

Apron: That portion of the stage which extends downstage of the curtain toward the audience.

Arches, 82, **83.**

Assembling scenery, 124-134.

Astrup Co., Inc., The, 54.

Backflaps, 61, 64. *See* Hinges.

Backings, 16, **33.**

Balustrades, **95,** 97.

Bar, wrecking, 50.

Battens, 13, **21,** 70, **99;** mending-, 64, 98; pipe-, **7,** 13, 134, 138, **139,** 140, **141;** stiffening-, **130,** 131.

Belaying pins, 7.

Bevel, sliding T-, 48.

Bits, 51.

Blocks, 7; corner-, 58, **73,** 74; profile-, 58, **73;** (pulleys), **7,** 65, 138, **139, 141,** 142; spacer-, 82, **83;** stop-, 126, **127.**

Bobbinet, 55.

Bolts, 61, 68, 71, 93, **95,** 98, **99,** 144, **145;** dead-, 85.

Bookcases, 90, **91.**

Boomerang, 104, 110, **121.**

Borders, **21, 33,** 36-38, 70, **99;** drapery, 13, 19, **21;** rigging, **21,** 22, **99,** 133, 140; wing-, **33,** 40.

·*Boyle, John & Co., Inc.,* 54.

Brace, -cleat, 64, **127,** 128, 146; corner-, 72, **73,** 75; -jack, **99,**

129; stage-, 64, **127,** 128; (tool), 51.

Bricks, **frontispiece, 111,** 122.

Brother Rat, 29, 36.

Brushes, paint, 103, **111;** paste, 52, **77;** varnish, 52.

Burlap, 94.

Bushes, 13, **33.**

Butt joint, 67, **69.**

Calsimine. *See* Kalsomine, 105.

Canvas, 54; repairs to, 98.

Canvassing, 71, 75-82, 94, 97, **99.**

Carbolic acid, 102.

Carpentry, 67, **69.**

Carriages, 94, **95.**

Casters, 66, 143, **145.**

Ceiling, 19, 22, 64, 84-85, 140, **141.**

Center-line, 27, **31,** 124.

Chain, 54, 70.

Chalk, 106, 119.

Charcoal, 106, 119.

Chicken wire, 54, 97, **99.**

Chisels, 49.

Clamps, brace-, 64; rigging, 66, 137.

Clancy, J. R. & Co., Inc., 59, 61, 63, 65, 66.

Cleats, brace-, 64, **127,** 128, 146; lash-, 64, 125, **127.**

Clenching plates, 50, **69,** 75.

Color, 101, 104, 106, **109.**

Convertible settings, **10,** 22, **31,** 36, 79, 151; painting, 122.

153

Corner, -blocks, 58, **73, 74**; -braces, 72, **73, 75**; -irons, 62, **69**; -plates, 62, **69**.

Cornices, 17, **91**, 93.

Corrugated, board, 55; fasteners, 60.

Cost, 1, 12, 22, 35, 47-66, 151.

Cotton batting, 55, 94.

Countersink, 68, 80, **81**; (tool), 51.

Counterweight system, 138, **139**.

Cover-flats, 94, **98**.

Curtains, 6, **7**.

Cut-outs, 13, 14, 82, **99**.

Cyclorama, 134; knuckles, 64, 134; settings, 13, **15**, 70, 151; sky, 9.

Cypress, 58.

Cyrano de Bergerac, 35.

Delta (circular saw), 49.

Design, 24-46.

Dodsworth, 36.

Doll's House, A, 29.

Dome, 9, 36.

Doorframes, **10, 15**, 19, 85, **87**, 132, 136.

Doors, **10**, 14, **15**, 19, 85, **87**, 92; flats, 79, **81**; running, 136.

Downstage, 5, **7**.

Draperies, 13, **15**, 18, 20, **21**, 53, 70, 133.

Drawing, 24-28, **43**, 45; equipment, 25.

Drills, 51, 52, 68.

Drop, leg- : A drop with its center cut out so that it becomes a border with a pair of wings attached.

Drops, 14, 71, **121**, 133, 140.

Duck, 54.

Dutchman: A term sometimes substituted for the words "stripper" and "jigger", q.v. Also applied to a special lens used in connection with lighting apparatus.

Elevations, 27, **43**.

Entrances, 22, 29.

Equipment, drawing, 25; painter's, 103; permanent, 6-9.

Exits, 22, 29.

Exterior sets, 22, 32, **33**, 36.

Faultless (casters), 66.

Feltdux (canvas), 54.

Files, 49.

Fir, 56.

Firebrand, The, 36.

Fireplaces, 30, 90, **91**.

First Lady, 16, 30, **31**, 36.

Fish-plate, 85, 98, **141**.

Flameproofing, 54, 98.

Flannel, 13, 20, 53.

Flat coat, 108.

Flats, 13, 71-82, 124-130; assigning, 41, **43**; cover-, 94, 98; number of, 18; numbering, 41, **73**; running, 135; sizes, 17-18.

Flies, 5, 14, 37.

Floating, 136.

Floor, -block, 138, **139**; plans, 26, **33, 39**, 45, 124; plates, 64, 129.

Fly gallery: A gallery from which the rigging system may be operated. Usually situated on one side wall about 20′ 0″ above the stage, and carrying a pin rail on its onstage edge. Its purpose is to save space on the stage floor.

Flying, 7, 136-143.

Footirons, 64, **99**, 131, 144, **145**.

Forestage: The part of the stage in front of the curtain. *See* Apron.

Fouling, 138.

Furniture, 28-32.

Gauze, 55.

Getaway (stairs and platforms), 32.

Glass, 54, 89.

Glue, canvassing, 59, 76, 79; size, 102, 106.

Grain, 68, 74, 80.

Graining, **frontispiece, 15, 111,** 118.

Grass mat: A mat made of raffia, used to simulate grass. May usually be borrowed from florists, window dressers or undertakers.

Gridiron (or grid), **7,** 8, 36, 137, **139,** 140.

Grommets, 70.

Ground-row, 16, **33, 99.**

Hammers, 50.

Hanger, -irons, 64, **130,** 143; picture frame-, 64, **130,** 133.

Hanging scenery, 133.

Hardware, 60-64.

High Tor, 32, **33.**

Hinges, 61, 64; doors, **87,** 88; flats, **77, 78;** joining with, **87, 99, 130,** 131, 132.

Hooks, lash-, 64, 126, **127;** S-, 64, **130,** 131, 133; wire, 62, 133.

Hue, 107, **109.**

Intensity, 107, **109.**

Interior sets, **15,** 20, **21,** 29-32, 151.

Iron, corner-, 62, **69;** foot-, 64, **99,** 131, 144, **145;** hanger-, 64, **130,** 143; sill, 63, 79, **81;** strap, 63, 80, **81.**

Jackknife stage: A scene-shifting device consisting of two large wagons, each carrying a complete scene. One wagon is pivoted near each tormentor. The scenes are set and struck by swinging one wagon offstage and the other on, like the blades of a jackknife.

Jacks, **99,** 129, 144-146.

Jiggers, **77, 78.**

Julius Caesar, 17.

Kalsomine, 105.

Keystone, 58, **73,** 74-75.

Knives, 49, 76, **77.**

Knots, **99, 127,** 137, **139.**

Knuckles, cyclorama, 64, 134.

L'Aiglon, 23.

Lash, -cleat, 64, 125, **127;** -hooks, 64, 126, **127;** -line, 125, **127.**

Lattice strip, 59, 82, 89.

Lazarus Laughed, 35.

Leaves, **33, 99, 111,** 122.

Level, 48.

Lighting, 34, 40, 117.

Liliom, 116.

Line, center-, 27, **31,** 124; lash-, 125, **127;** purchase-, 138, **139;** rigging, 6-8, 137-140; sight-, 36-40; snatch-, **130,** 137-143; stopper-, **139,** 140; tormentor-, 27, **31, 39,** 124.

Lining, **111,** 118; snap-, 119, **121.**

Lip, **81,** 82, 124.

Loading platform, **139,** 140.

Lock, 63, **87;** -rail, 138, **139.**

Lumber, 55-59.

Mantel, **10,** 30, 90, **91.**

Marble, 116.

Markwell (stapling machine), 50.

Masking, 6, 36-40.

Materials, 12, 53-66; paint, 103-106.

Men in White, 36.

Mending, -battens, 64, 98; -plates, 62, **69.**

Miter, 68, **69;** box, 49, **69.**

Models, 28, 143, 147.

Molding, 59, **91,** 92, 93, 96, **117.**

Muslin, 14, 54, 82, 86.

Nails, 60, **69, 73,** 125.

Needle, 52, 97.

Netting, 70; poultry, 54, 97, **99.**

Noelting Co. (casters), 66.

Nosing, 96.

Nuts, 63.

Offstage, 6.

Onstage, 6.

Padding, 55, 94, 96.

Paddles, stirring, 104.

Pails, 104.

Paint, 104; bins, 104; preparing, 102; shop, 103. *See* Pigments.

Painter's Terms, The, 107.

Painting, 101-123; blending, 116; bricks, **frontispiece**, 111, 122; convertible sets, 122; corrections, 115; dry brushing, **111**, 112, 118; equipment, 103; flat coat, 108; leaves, **111**, 122; lining, **111**, 118; plaster, 117; scrumbling, **111**, 112; shadowing, 117, 122; spattering, 110, **111**, 114-118; sponging, 112, 117; stone, **15**, **33**, 121; texture, 116; wallpaper, 120, **121**; woodwork, **15**, **111**, 118. *See* Pigments.

Panels, **10**, 86, **91**, 92, 118.

Papier-mâché, 93.

Parallel: A platform of complicated construction. Used by professionals because of its lightness. *See Scenery for the Theatre.*

Paste, 59, 78; brush, 52, **77**.

Peer Gynt, 14.

Pencils, 26, 106.

Piano wire, **21**, 22, 62, 63.

Picture frame-hangers, 64, **130**, 133.

Pigments, 104-106; mixing, 101-103, **109**.

Pin rail, 7, 137, **139**.

Pine, ponderosa, 58; white, 57; yellow, 56.

Pipe, 65; -battens, **7**, 13, 134, 138, **139**, 140, **141**.

Plane, principle, 12; (tool), 49.

Plans, floor, 26, **31**, **39**, 45, 124.

Plaster, back wall, 8; painting, 117.

Plates, ceiling-, 64, 85, **141**; clenching, 50, **69**, **75**; corner-, 62, **69**; fish-, 85, 98, **141**; floor, 64, 129; mending-, 62, **69**.

Platforms, 14, 19, 32, **33**, 93-**95**; loading, **139**, 140; models, 28, 143; rolling, 143, **145**.

Pliers, 52.

Plugging, **10**, 80, **81**.

Plumb bob, 48.

Plywood, 55, 86.

Poultry netting, 54, 97, **99**.

Practical: Adjective used to describe any scene-unit or property which can actually be used. A practical tree can be climbed. A practical lamp can be lighted.

Profile, -blocks, 58, **73**; board, 55.

Projector, opaque, 119.

Properties (or props): All items visible to the audience except scenery, lights, and costumes. If intended to be carried onstage by the actors they are called "hand props."

Proscenium, 5, **7**; inner, 6, **7**, 37.

Pulleys, **7**, 65, 138, **139**, **141**, 142. *See* Block.

Pump, 104.

Punch, center, 52; sureshot, 51.

Purchase line, 138, **139**.

Rails, flat, 72, **73**; lock-, 138, **139**; pin, 7, 137, **139**; stair, **95**, 97; window, **10**, **87**, 89.

Ramps, 16.

Rasp, 49.

Reaming, 68.

Repairs, 98.

Return: A type of supplementary tormentor, placed upstage of the regular tormentor and painted to match the set. Used with interior sets it permits the lights to shine onstage from behind the tormentor. Used with exterior sets it provides a downstage entrance.

Rigging, 7, 137-143; supplies, 65, 66.

Risers, 19, 94, **95**.

Rocks, **33**, 96, 98.
Rolling, 143-146.
Romeo and Juliet, 38.
Rope, 65.
Ropeline system, 7, 137, 138, **139**.
Rosine : A flexible glue used for applying netting, metallic powders, and metal foil to drops and borders.
Rule, 47.
Running, 135.

S-hooks, 64, **130**, 131, 133.
Salvage, 12, 22, 68.
Sandbags, 66, 137.
Sash, **10**, **87**, 89 ; cord, 65, 125 ; tool, 103.
Sawing, 67, **69**.
Saws, 48, 49.
Scale, 26-28, **37**, 124, 143, 148.
Scene Technician's Handbook, vii.
Scene-units, **10**, 11, 13-20.
Scenery, assembling, 124-134; building, 67-100; design of, 24-46; dismantling, 68; economy, 20-23; hung, 70, 133; nature of, 11-23; painting, 101-123; shifting, 135-150; simplicity of, 1-4; stock, 16-20; washing, 123.
Scenery for the Theatre, viii, 71, 75, 146.
Screen, wire, 54, 89.
Screw eyes, **21**, 22, 62.
Screwdrivers, 50, 51.
Screws, 61, 68, 75, 80; stage-, 64, 128, 131, **145**.
Scrim, 55.
Scrumbling, **111**, 112.
Sections, 27.
Set (verb), 135, 148.
Set-piece : Any scene-unit made to stand alone in the center of the stage.
Settings, convertible, **10**, 22, **31**, 36, 79, 122, 151; cyclorama, 13, **15**, 70, 151; economy, 20-23; exterior, 22, 32, **33**, 36; interior, **15**, 20, **21**, 29-32, 151 ; minimum, 20, **21**.
Shadows, 117, 122.
She Loves Me Not, 38.
Sheaves, 7, 65, 138.
Shift, card, 149 ; chart, 147 ; scene, 35, 135-150.
Sight-lines, 36-40.
Sill, 86, **87**, 89 ; irons, 63, 79, **81**.
Size, 102, 106.
Sketches, 27, 45.
Skull, The, 35.
Sky, 9, 14 ; cyclorama, 9.
Snap-lining, 119, **121**.
Snaps, harness, 62.
Snatch-lines, **130**, 137-143.
Snips, 49.
Spacer-blocks, 82, **83**.
Spatter, 110, **111**, 114-118.
Special, 22, 151.
Spindle, 85.
Sponging, 112, 117.
Spreaders, **7**, 8, 90, **91**.
Spruce, 56.
Squares, 48, **69**, **95**.
Squaring, 67, **69**, 72, **95**.
Stage, 5-9, 34 ; carpenter, 149; down- and up-, 5, **7** ; -hand, 146-150 ; house, 5, **7** ; left and right, 5 ; off- and on-, 6 ; -screws, 64, 128, 131, **145** ; weight, **69**, 129.
Stage, revolving : A disc stage, similar to a wagon but pivoted in the center. Used to facilitate quick scene changes.
Stairs, 14, 19, 94-97 ; rail, **95**, 97 ; getaway, 32.
Staples, 50 ; poultry netting, 54, 97.
Stapling machine, 50.
Stencil, 120, **121**.
Steps, 14, 19, 94-97 ; getaway steps, 32.
Stiffener, 85, **141**.
Stiles, 72, **73** ; inner, 79, **81** ; window, **10**, **87**, 89.
Stock, 34 ; scenery, 16-20, 40-43.
Stone, **15**, **33**, 121. .

Stopper-line, **139**, 140.
Stops, 142.
Stove, 104; bolts, 61, **99**, 144, **145**.
Stovepipe wire, 63, 97.
Strap iron, 63, 80, **81**.
Stretchers, 84, **141**.
Strike, 135, 148, 149.
Strippers, **77**, 78.
Strips, edging, 94, 96; lattice, 59, 82, 89.
Strut, 82, **83**.
Stucco, 112, 117.
Sweeps, 79, 82, **83**.

Tacker, 50.
Tacks, 50, 61, 75, **77**, 79.
Tape, friction, 65, **99**, 137, **139**; twilled, **15**, 55, 89.
Teaser, 6, **7**, 17, 38; -thickness, **39**, 40.
Texture, 116.
Thickness, 16, 82, **83**; teaser-, **39**, 40; tormentor-, 38, **39**.
Thor (power drills), 51.
Tie off, 126, **127**, **139**.
Tin snips, 49.
Tip-jack, 144, **145**.
Toggle-bar, 72, **73**, 78, 79, **81**, 85, **87**, **130**, 131.
Tones, 107, **109**.
Tools, 47-52.
Tormentors, 6, **7**; -line, 27, **31**, **39**, 124; -thickness, 38, **39**.
Tracks (curtain), 6.
Traps, 9.
Treads, 19, 94-96.
Trees, 14, 22, **33**, 97, **99**.
Trim, 92-93.
Trimble & Fink Mfg. Co., 51.
Tripping: On stages with grid-irons 20′ 0″ to 30′ 0″ high, a drop is sometimes rigged with two sets of lines, one for each batten. By raising the lower batten to the level of the upper batten, the drop is folded in half and can then be flown out of sight-lines. This process is called "trip-ping" the drop.
Turnbuckle, **21**, *22*, 62.
Turnbuttons, *62*, **81**.

Unit, scene-, **10**, 11, 13-20.
Upstage, 5, **7**.

Value, 107, **109**.
Varnish, 59; brush, **52**.
Velours, 6.
Velvet, 6, 13, 54.
Vise, 52.

Wagons, 144, **145**.
Walking down (up), 136.
Wallboard, 55.
Wallpaper, 120, **121**.
Walls, 16; back, 5, **7**, 8, 20, **21**, **130**, 142; curved, 79, **83**; side, 5, **7**, **21**.
Washers, 61.
Washing scenery, 123.
Webbing, 70.
White pine, 57.
Windows, **10**, 14, **15**, 19, 30, **87**, 89; flats, 79, **81**.
Wing, 16; -border, **33**, 40; -nuts, 63.
Wings, 5, 16, 37.
Wire, hooks, 62, 133; netting, 54, 97, **99**; piano, **21**, *22*, 62, 63; screen, 54, 89; stovepipe, 63, 97.
Women, The, 18.
Wood, 56 (*see* Lumber); ply-, 55, 86; rasp, 49.
Wood wing: The most common type of wing; cut out and painted to represent trees and shrubbery.
Working through, 108.
Wrecking bar, 50.
Wrench, pipe, 52.

Yellow Jack, 23.
Yellow pine, 56.
You Can't Take It with You, 29.
You Never Can Tell, 35.